RESPECT TRAINING
for Puppies

MICHELE WELTON

Disclaimer

This book is intended to provide general information about dog training. I have not personally evaluated your dog and therefore the advice contained in this book may not be applicable to your particular dog. The author and publisher make no representations or warranties about the accuracy, applicability, or completeness of the information in this book, and assume no liability for any consequences, loss, or damage caused or alleged to be caused by the information in this book.

About the Author

Hello! I'm Michele Welton and I have over 40 years of experience as a Dog Trainer, Obedience Instructor, Dog Breed Consultant, founder of three Dog Training Centers, and author of 17 books.

I've trained and shown dogs in competitive obedience, agility, herding, tracking, and Schutzhund.

My advice on choosing, raising, and training dogs has been featured on the Orange County TV News Channel and in the *Orange County Register* in Southern California.

Visit my website at
https://www.yourpurebredpuppy.com

Table of Contents

Chapter 1

Thirty Seconds to a Calm, Polite, Well-Behaved Puppy

Thirty seconds?

Yes, thirty seconds. Bear with me for a moment and I'll explain.

Many people think that **obedience training** is the key to making a pup well-behaved. They hope that by taking their pup to a one-hour obedience class each week and then practicing the commands for another hour each night, their pup will be well-behaved.

But the truth is that **very little** obedience training needs to be done with a puppy to get him to be well-behaved.

That's right. **Very little** obedience training.

Keep in mind that I've instructed obedience classes for over 35 years, so I certainly wouldn't say that unless it was true.

The truth is that what a puppy needs most is to be **lived with properly.** Living with a pup properly includes *some* obedience training, yes. And we'll cover obedience training in this book.

But teaching commands such as "Sit" or "Lie down" only influences about 20% of the way your pup ends up behaving.

On the other hand, **how you live with the puppy around the house on a daily basis** influences 80% of his behavior.

Puppy training is really about Teachable Moments–very short moments–all through the day

You train your puppy *in quick moments throughout the day* as the pup tries various behaviors and you give either a thumbs-up or a thumbs-down. I'll be showing you how to do that.

 Those **quick interactions** around the house, outside in the yard, feeding and grooming, and taking your puppy for a walk, determine how your pup will turn out.

 Those **quick interactions** are how your puppy learns how high (or low) your expectations are, and whether your rules carry any weight or you're just blowing smoke.

 Those **quick interactions** are how you mold your puppy into a calm, polite, well-behaved dog…or an excitable, disrespectful, misbehaving dog. It's really up to you.

Those quick interactions take only thirty seconds.
Often *far* less than thirty seconds.

Let me give you an example from my own family. One of my current dogs is a Poodle. Another is a Chihuahua. The Poodle is very smart and learns quickly— she knows about a hundred commands.

The Chihuahua is not very smart and learns more slowly—she knows six commands.

Yet both dogs are equally housebroken, attentive and obedient, calm and well-behaved, and trustworthy with other people and other animals. Because they were both *raised* right, you see.

 When they were puppies, I took advantage of 30-second opportunities to show them exactly what they should be doing from the moment they woke up in the morning to the moment they went to sleep at night. I filled their days with predictable routines so they learned exactly *how* I expected them to live with me.

Whether they were eating a meal, getting brushed, going out to potty, playing a game with me, or going for a walk—we had a routine for everything. Predictable structure is so important to puppies!

 I also set firm boundaries that certain behaviors were *not* allowed. Dogs want to know what they *should* do, but also what they *shouldn't* do.

 And I established the right human-canine relationship in which *I* was the calm, confident, trusted leader and *they* were the calm, confident, trusting followers.

> If you do just those three things—properly—with your puppy, you'll have no problems with him. Even if he knows only a few obedience commands, he'll turn into a great adult dog.

On the other hand, many people dutifully take their pup to a year's worth of obedience classes, only to become frustrated because he is still chewing things, jumping on the kids, chasing the cat, and barking.

That's because in obedience class, owners are not taught how to interact with their pup around the house every day. And it's those interactions that will make or break how your puppy turns out.

Puppies learn things every minute they're awake.

Puppies learn *all the time.* You can't stop them from learning things.

Every time you do something with your puppy, he learns something about you. Every time he tries a behavior, he learns something from your reaction…or your non-reaction.

The question is, WHAT has your pup learned from you?

Here are some examples of behaviors that puppies learn, in 30 seconds, from your reaction or non-reaction:

- "Barking gets me out of my crate."

- "Whining makes people give me things from their dinner plate."

- "Behind the sofa is a secret place to pee."

- "The kids keep chewable toys in their bedrooms."

- "The laundry room is full of smelly underwear I can chew on."

- "The bathroom wastebasket includes used tissues I can shred and swallow."

- "The stuffing comes out of cushions so easily."

- "Jumping on people makes them pet me."

- "If I don't want to give up my toy, I can clamp down on it with my teeth and hold on."

- "I can run away from people pretty fast."

- "When people reach toward my collar, I can dodge them for quite some time."

- "Pushing my head into someone's lap makes them pet me."

- "Pulling on the leash makes people follow me."

- "If I don't want my nails clipped or my teeth brushed, I can make it stop by squirming and struggling."

Puppies learn things even while *you're* sleeping.

Say you're asleep and your pup is wandering around the house. He finds the bowl of potato chips you left on the coffee table, within easy reach of his paws.

Did you just teach him something? Heck, yes! You taught him that nighttime is not a time to sleep, but to search for food.

You taught him that food is fair game if he can reach it. You taught him that you can't correct him when you're not present.

See how much you taught him while you were sleeping?

> Again, puppy training is much less about the teaching of commands and much more about *how you live with your pup.*

Virtually ALL canine behaviors (good and bad) are created by the way you live with the puppy.

What you do with him…what you don't do with him…what you allow him to do…these are all messages to your puppy.

Send the right messages and you will have no problems with your pup. Send the wrong messages and you will have problems. It's that simple. *How you live with your puppy every day* is what dictates how he will behave in your family. Not a bunch of obedience commands.

Chapter 2

All a Dog Needs is Love?

The internet is full of claims about dogs, and one of the most common claims I see is this: "All a dog needs is love."

Now, is that true or false?

Surprise! It's true. All a dog needs is love.

Presuming that you're defining *love* properly! The problem is that many people equate *love* with *affection* (petting, stroking, hugs, kisses, sweet talk). With this improper definition in mind, owners bring home a puppy and proceed to shower him with affection.

Now, affection is certainly *part* of love—but when it comes to canines, affection is only a small part of love. A very small part.

Truly loving a dog means providing what the dog *really* needs—and that might be quite different than what you want to give him.

Owners who want to spoil a puppy, coddle a puppy, allow naughty behaviors, hug and kiss a puppy, or curl up on the sofa endlessly stroking and cuddling a puppy…are providing what *they* want to give the puppy. Not what the puppy really needs.

In fact, the very things that some owners want to give their pup are the exact opposite of what the pup really needs. If you truly want to love your puppy, and certainly if you want to avoid or solve behavior problems, you need to provide what he really needs.

True love means providing your pup with:

 a structured life filled with predictable patterns and routines, so the puppy feels secure that he always knows what will happen next.

 consistent positive and negative consequences, so the pup can make good decisions about which behaviors he should do, and which behaviors he shouldn't do.

 calm, confident leadership, so the puppy recognizes that you're in charge and looks trustingly to you for guidance and direction.

You can't claim to love a dog without providing those three things. Every dog craves them. Every dog thrives on them.

In summary, *loving a dog* is much more than just giving affection.

> If an owner is showering tons of affection upon her dog, but her leadership is weak, her daily routines are weak, and her positive and negative consequences are weak, she and the pup are going to struggle with behavioral issues directly resulting from (ironically) a lack of true love.

Chapter 3

Do These 3 Things and Your Pup's Behavior Will Be (Nearly) Perfect

Now, no one (human or canine) is perfect! But your pup's behavior will be *nearly* perfect if you do 3 things.

First, provide a structured life filled with routines.

Dogs thrive on **sameness,** routines that are familiar, predictable, repeated. As much as possible, do the same things with your puppy every day—the same things in the same order, using the same words.

Also show your pup what you expect **him** to do as **his** part of the routine. Once he learns the routine for, say, meal time, if you do your part, he will do his part. Automatically. Day in and day out.

The trick is to make sure the routines your puppy is learning are **good** ones that lead to good behavior. If he learns **bad** routines, he will repeat them just as readily! The vast majority of behavior problems in dogs are caused by the owner (inadvertently) teaching the pup bad routines.

In this book, we're going to create good routines that cover bed time, wake-up time, meal time, play time, walk time, grooming time, potty breaks, and so on. Dogs feel most secure when their life is structured and predictable.

Second, provide positive and negative consequences.

Dogs are opportunists, which means they're always on the lookout for *opportunities* to get something good for themselves.

If you add a reward (a positive consequence) to a behavior you want your puppy to do (greeting guests politely, standing still while you brush him, going to the bathroom in the right place), he's more likely to repeat that behavior.

On the flip side, dogs try to avoid doing things that make them feel uncomfortable or unhappy. If you attach a negative consequence to a behavior you **don't** want him to do (jumping on people, barking, chasing the cat), he'll avoid repeating that behavior.

Your puppy needs both thumbs-up and thumbs-down feedback so he will make good choices.

We call this **Balanced** Training, where you reward the good and correct the bad. Sometimes it's called **Yes & No** Training because you tell your pup *Yes* for some behaviors, and *No* for others. It's the perfect training method for canines, matching the commonsense way they learn.

But isn't it "mean" to correct a dog?

Absolutely not. Corrections give your puppy valuable information about the behaviors that you don't want him to do. How else is he to know?

There is a dog training philosophy called *positive reinforcement ONLY* (or *purely positive*). It starts with the exact same positive reinforcement that I use—praise, food, petting, toys, and gentle guidance with your hands or the leash.

So far, so good! But there's a reason it's called *positive ONLY*, and this is where the wheels come off the wagon.

With *positive ONLY* training, no matter how bad a dog's behavior is (knocking people over by jumping, barking, lunging at other dogs), you don't correct it with *anything* that might make the dog feel uncomfortable or "sad"—not even for a moment, and not even if doing so would completely eradicate the bad behavior so that it never came up again.

Some *positive ONLY* trainers won't even say "No."

Imagine if we raised our kids that way.

No, if you want your pup to STOP doing something—stop pulling on the leash, stop jumping on people, stop lunging toward other dogs, stop barking, stop stealing food, stop chasing the cat...

...positive ONLY doesn't work.

Think about it. What happens when you want your pup to stop chasing a cat and come to you, but at that particular moment he's not hungry and would RATHER chase the cat than munch on a biscuit?

> Owners who rely on *positive ONLY* training are stuck whenever their puppy "isn't in the mood" to do something, or even more importantly, to STOP doing something.

An old trainer once remarked that if a dog really wants to chase a cat, he will chase it "regardless of biscuits showering upon him like manna from heaven."

So if you've watched some YouTube videos that claim you can teach your dog to stop jumping on people by teaching him to sit, they're quite wrong.

If a pup likes to jump on people, and you simply teach him how to sit for a treat—without correcting the jumping—he learns that sitting brings him a treat, sure. But he also doesn't forget how much he enjoys jumping! So at any given time, you can never know whether he will choose the treat or the fun of jumping.

If both behaviors bring him a reward, how is he supposed to choose? Flip a coin? His behavior ends up depending on which reward he wants most at that moment.

In fact, when you think about it, if your puppy jumps on someone and you pull him off and coax him to sit and then give him a treat, you're **rewarding** him for jumping. Remember how quickly puppies learn patterns: "First I jump. Then I sit and get a treat. Therefore, to get a treat, I must start by jumping!" Ugh.

> No, if you want your puppy to **not jump,** don't add positive consequences anywhere close to the jumping behavior, else you'll get **more** jumping. If you want **less** jumping, you add a negative consequence. Once he demonstrates that he won't jump any more, bring out the treats and teach him to sit.

> Balanced training (positive and negative consequences) makes logical sense to your puppy. He **wants** to know—**needs** to know—what happens if he does *A* and what happens if he does *B*. Then he can make the sensible choice.

Third, be a calm, confident leader.

Show your puppy that you're in control of everything in his life, that everything good comes from you, and that he should look to you for guidance and direction. Then he will be happy to be a respectful follower.

Dogs are born with an instinctive desire to belong to a *social group* (a family or pack).

When a puppy joins your family, even if your family is only the two of you, his instincts compel him to seek out its structure:

 Who is the leader who sets the boundaries?

 Who are the followers who follow the leader?

Dogs don't want to be leaders.

The vast majority of puppies don't want to be leaders. They really, really don't want to be leaders. They're much happier as followers.

But a dog isn't comfortable in a world where *no one* seems to be in charge.

So if you're not comfortable providing guidance and direction and setting firm boundaries, if you feel guilty about saying "No" to your pup and making it stick…well, that's not going to sit well with your pup and he will probably try to assume the leadership role himself.

That doesn't mean he's a "dominant" dog with ambitions to rule your household. It doesn't mean he **wants** to be in charge. It just means that he knows how important it is that **someone** be in charge.

Since you've fallen down on the job, he's trying to fill that role for you.

If your puppy is the leader

When you fail to act like a leader, you'll see behavior problems when you try to get him to do something he doesn't want to do.

He might bark back at you. He might struggle when you try to restrain him or clip his nails or brush his teeth. He might resist being picked up or growl when you try to take a toy away. He might not come when you call him (assuming that you've already taught him what *Come* means).

Since you haven't shown him that you're the one making the decisions, he doesn't understand why he has to do what you say.

Your lack of leadership jeopardizes your pup's health and safety because there will be times in his life when you'll need to do things that he doesn't understand and doesn't enjoy:

 give him medicine that tastes awful

 remove something from his mouth

 roll him over to pluck a disgusting tick off his belly

Your puppy can't understand that medicines will help him, that things he picks up from the ground might poison him or choke him, that ticks carry disease and must be removed. Without this knowledge, your pup doesn't know what's best for him.

For his own safety, he has to accept **your** greater knowledge and judgment in every aspect of his life. But he will only do that if he trusts your leadership.

Does your puppy view you as his trusted leader?

- When visitors come to the door, does your pup bark a warning, but then look at you, expecting you to take over and handle the situation? That's trusting you as the leader. Or does he rush the door and pitch an ongoing fit, making his own decision about how to deal with this visitor?

- When you're ready to go for a walk and you open the door or gate, does your pup wait for your permission to go through? That's showing polite respect for you as the leader. Or does he lunge through the door or gate the moment it opens, oblivious to your presence at the other end of the leash?

- Does your pup walk nicely on a loose leash, glancing at you regularly to see which direction you want to go in? That's recognizing you as the leader. Or does he pull you around and make his own decisions to go left or right, fast or slow?

- When a stranger or a strange dog approaches, does your pup look at you, expecting you to handle the situation? That's trusting you as the leader. Or does he make his own decision to bark and pull and lunge at other people or other dogs?

> You are your puppy's caregiver. Your relationship with him should be one where he is taught to look trustingly at you for guidance, direction, and permission. That's the relationship that every dog thrives on.

How to establish yourself as the leader

You demonstrate leadership by simply interacting with your puppy in the specific ways that I explain in this book.

Establish good patterns and routines that govern everything your pup does.

 Teach him to be calm and to look to you for guidance, direction, and permission.

 Make yourself *important*—the most important thing—in your puppy's life. Encourage him to look at you and come *toward* you. Step up and be the decision-maker. Show him the clear, black-and-white rules and routines he is to follow, and then make sure he does.

These simple actions are viewed *by your puppy* as the actions of a leader. If you follow the chapters faithfully, the result will be a calm, well-behaved pup who loves, trusts, AND respects you.

Chapter 4

(Cheat Sheet): How to Use Routines, Consequences, and Leadership in Daily Living

> The easiest way to train your puppy is to establish choreographed routines—same things, same order, same words—with yourself as the director, the one in charge. Create good routines, stick to them, and your pup's behavior will be predictable and good.

 When your puppy does something you don't like, say "No" or "AH-ah" along with a corrective technique that discourages him from repeating that behavior. (Chapter 5)

 When your puppy does something you **do** like, let him know by saying, "Good" or "Yes" along with a reward that encourages him to repeat the behavior. (Chapter 8)

Indoors, require **calm** behavior. Pups who are allowed to be excitable indoors are far more likely to have behavior problems. Don't allow running around the house, rough play, barking, jumping, rushing the doorbell, or attacking the vacuum cleaner. If necessary, have the pup wear his leash indoors so you can stop those behaviors. (Chapter 9)

 Whenever your puppy is on leash, the leash must be kept nice and loose. If he is currently pulling on the leash during walks, **don't go for any more walks** until you've taught him to stop pulling in your own home and yard. (Chapter 10–11)

 Teach him to go into his crate or pen and to stay there quietly, with no excitability or barking. (Chapter 13)

 Don't let your puppy go through open doors or gates without your permission. It's a subtle way to get him looking to YOU for guidance and direction. (Chapter 15)

 Teach your pup to go to his dog bed when told, and **to stay there until given permission to get up.** This valuable exercise teaches calmness, impulse control, and physical and mental relaxation. Every pup should be able to do it. (Chapter 16)

 When you call your puppy, make sure he comes every single time. For now, that might mean keeping him on a leash in the house and a long cord in the yard, so you can get hold of him to make sure he comes. (Chapter 18)

 Make sure he takes food and toys gently from your hand. Don't let him have anything if he grabs at it. (Chapter 19)

When you prepare his meals, keep him in the kitchen with you. You want him to see that his food comes from you. Don't let him race around or bark. He should wait politely. Have him *Sit* before you place his bowl on the floor. To discourage picky eating, give him 10 minutes to eat, then pick up his bowl. (Chapter 20)

 If he has any behavioral issues, he should not be allowed on furniture unless invited up. Sleeping on human beds or furniture is a privilege that must be earned. (Chapter 21)

 Don't let your pup demand lots of petting and attention. This can create psychologically unhealthy (bossy or needy) dogs. **You** decide when to pet and when to stop. *That's enough* is an important lesson for all puppies to learn. (Chapter 22)

 Stop all mouthing or nipping at anyone's hands or feet. (Chapter 23)

 Barking makes dogs more excitable. Don't allow your puppy to bark at harmless things such as your neighbor or your neighbor's dog. Certainly he can bark to alert you to something, but he should stop barking when told. He should be quiet when left home alone. (Chapter 24)

 Don't allow jumping on anyone, including yourself. (Chapter 25)

 Don't allow your puppy to "rush the doorbell", i.e., pitch a fit when someone comes to the door. (Chapter 26)

Make sure your pup will move out of your way when told. (Chapter 27)

 Teach your puppy to *Sit* and to stay sitting until you cue him to get up. (Chapter 31)

 Don't let your puppy fuss when you're brushing him, bathing him, clipping his nails, or brushing his teeth. Teach him to accept handling of any part of his body. (Chapter 32)

 Teach your pup to give or drop whatever is in his mouth when told. (Chapter 33)

 Begin a proven housebreaking program where your puppy can only go to the bathroom in the right place. (Chapter 34)

 Make sure he greets people and other animals politely, or else ignores them. Don't allow him to act excitably, aggressively, or fearfully toward people or other dogs. (Chapter 43–44)

 Make sure your puppy is respectful of other pets in your family. He may not take anything away from another pet. He should "take turns" for treats and attention. No bickering, pestering, pushiness, or jealousy. (Chapter 46–47)

 If you follow the program in this book, your pup should grow up being able to do everything in the list above.

You can start teaching these skills at any age.

Just don't expect quick results in pups under 10 weeks old. With these canine infants, focus on mouthing/biting (Chapter 23), crate training (Chapter 13) and potty training (Chapter 34).

You can teach these skills in any order.

I teach whatever happens to come up during the day. But if your pup isn't 100% housebroken, start with Chapter 34.

You don't need to teach just one thing at a time.

For example, you can introduce "Good" and "No", being quiet in the crate, walking on a leash, come when called, wait at the door, and so on. As you read each chapter, implement the routines and techniques in that chapter as soon as possible.

It's easier to train a dog if your other dogs are already well-behaved.

If your other dogs have behavioral issues, if they sometimes listen and sometimes not, or if they're not 100% housebroken, a puppy is likely to follow their unruly behaviors.

It's easier to train a puppy when you're home most of the day.

 First, because dogs are *social* animals who want to be close to their family during the day. When a pup's social needs are being met, training is easier.

 Second, when you interact with your puppy frequently throughout the day, these micro-interactions give you the chance *to respond to everything the pup does.* The more often you can do this, the faster the puppy learns.

But if everyone works or goes to school, you can't reward good behavior or correct bad behavior. The longer a behavior goes without correction, the more habitual it becomes.

When someone finally does come home, the puppy races around with wild excitement. It's harder to encourage calmness in a lonely, bored pup whose social needs are not being met.

It's easier to train a puppy who is getting enough exercise.
Dogs are active, bright animals. If they don't have anything to do except wander aimlessly around the yard, they feel bored and frustrated. Pups vent boredom and frustration by destroying things, barking, or being rambunctious.

> It's harder to make a dog conform to *your* expectations when *his* needs aren't being met. Yes, you need to stop him from destroying things and barking (I'll explain how), but you should also add more exercise and interesting activities to his life.

It's easier to train some breeds than other breeds.

Someone who has never trained a dog before will find it easier to train the average Golden Retriever or Sheltie or Poodle, compared with the average Basenji or Shiba or Bull Terrier.

Look up your breed on my website (yourpurebredpuppy.com). A challenging breed is definitely trainable, but you'll probably need to put in a lot more time and effort.

It's easier to train a puppy when you use a balanced training method.

Balanced Training is a time-tested training method that rewards good behavior AND corrects bad behavior. This clearly communicates to your puppy what you want him to do and not do. It's sensible, fair, and easy to understand—the perfect training method for dogs.

It's easier to train a puppy when you teach ALL the skills...

...rather than cherry-picking some and blowing off the rest.

For example, you might be tempted to focus on commands (such as "Come" and "Lie down") while still allowing your pup to race around indoors, bark at visitors, jump on people, demand petting and attention, and pull on the leash.

That's not going to work. Allowing excitable, impulsive, or disrespectful **behavior** keeps a puppy in an excitable, impulsive, and disrespectful **mind-set.** This state of mind is stressful for a puppy to live with and virtually guarantees more behavior problems in the future.

> So commit to working on each skill on the list. They're all important in encouraging calm and respectful behavior and discouraging excitable and disrespectful behavior.

Chapter 5

Teaching "No"

When you tell your puppy "No", you want him to learn:

- that this particular behavior is not allowed

- that he must stop the behavior

- that he should not repeat it

Have you already taken your pup to an obedience class? If so, you might have been told that you should stop him from doing something by *redirecting* his attention from an undesirable behavior to a better behavior.

For example, he's chewing on your hand. You're told to pick up a toy and wiggle it on the floor so that he switches his attention to the toy. Now he's biting on something appropriate instead of your hand.

Alternatively, you're told to *remove* whatever the puppy is acting inappropriately toward. For example, he's stealing used tissues from the wastebasket beside the sofa. You're told to move the wastebasket out of his reach. Or remove the pup from the room.

> *Redirection* and *removal* work okay with very young puppies who have a short attention span and an "out of sight, out of mind" way of thinking. These techniques might also be effective with some older pups and even some very sensitive adult dogs.

Unfortunately, those are often the ONLY "corrective" techniques that owners are taught...and those techniques will eventually fail.

At some point—guaranteed—your puppy will be so determined to bark, chase the cat, mouth your hand, jump on people, charge the door when the doorbell rings, etc. that he ignores your attempts at redirection and removal.

And honestly, how far can you go with this, anyway?

- When your arms are black and blue from his "playful" nips, should you keep waving a toy in Puppy's face hoping to get him to bite it instead?

- Should you remove the Christmas tree because Puppy keeps pulling off the ornaments? Perhaps you should remove the pup by banishing him to the basement? One family suspended their Christmas tree from the ceiling so their dog couldn't reach it. Ugh.

Or should you simply teach him to STOP doing certain things?
You can probably tell that my answer is "Yes, you should teach him to stop doing certain things."

In fact, handing your puppy a toy or a treat when he's chewing on your hand simply rewards him for chewing on your hand. Puppies repeat behaviors that bring them a reward. Not exactly what you want to do, is it?

At some point, every puppy needs to learn the meaning of "No" and "AH-ah."

All parents and grandparents recognize the sound "AH-ah!" It's an abrupt guttural sound that comes out of our mouths instinctively when a toddler does something alarming.

Now I don't mean a *gentle sing-song admonishment* ("ah-ah-AHHH") that you might use with a child who is reaching for a cookie before supper.

I mean the sharp, shocked, alarmed "AH-ah!" that bursts out of your mouth when the child is reaching toward a hot stove!

"AH-ah" has a couple of advantages over "No."

 "AH-ah" bursts from your throat more quickly than you can form your lips around "No." Make it a quick, choppy, urgent sound. Think of the toddler's hand so close to the hot stove!

 "AH-ah" may be a better word to use than "No" if you've been saying "No" to your pup for a long time and he has developed the habit of ignoring it. It can be a good idea to start fresh with "AH-ah", adding the corrective techniques I'll be teaching you in this book.

I use both words interchangeably so my dogs learn both words.

> Try not to use your pup's name when you say "No" or "AH-ah" so he doesn't associate his name with anything negative. However, if you have multiple dogs, you might need to use the name of the guilty one so the innocent one doesn't feel reprimanded.

You might be thinking, "But I say 'No' all the time, yet my puppy doesn't stop what he's doing!"

That's right, if all you do is SAY it, it won't mean a thing to your puppy. He wasn't born understanding that our sounds have meaning. To a dog, *no* is just a sound, no more meaningful than a whistling teakettle. *No* is meaningless until you show your puppy that it means **"Stop—not allowed."**

Puppies learn language just as babies do. You hold up a teddy bear to your baby and say "teddy." Now imagine if you repeated "teddy" but never held up the bear. How would the baby know what that sound means? Words are only meaningless sounds until you connect the sound with an object or action.

You actually have experience with this. When you listen to a conversation in an unfamiliar language, everything sounds like one long, fast, run-on sentence, doesn't it? You can't even tell where one word ends and the next begins.

But if you don't speak French and a gentleman from France repeated "pom" while showing you an apple, you'd get it. You may not know how to spell it (it's actually *pomme*), but you would understand that the SOUND *pom* refers to the red fruit.

> In the same way, use short simple sounds with your puppy: *come, ball, sit.* Don't bury the key word in a barrage of other sounds. And immediately connect that keyword to the appropriate object or action. In other words, don't ask your pup if he wants *supper,* then withhold it for 10 minutes!

Back to the sound *No* and how to make it mean something.

Say "No" **AS** your puppy is doing something you don't want (barking, jumping, chewing on the table leg, pestering the cat).

A second or two later, add a *corrective technique* that actually makes him stop the behavior. I'll give you examples in a minute.

When you're first teaching your puppy what *No* means, never say the sound **without also** doing the corrective technique.

Because in the beginning, it's the corrective technique—not the sound *No*—that makes your puppy stop the behavior.

But since you're pairing the sound **with** the corrective technique, at some point you'll be able to say "No" and your puppy will stop whatever he's doing so quickly that you won't have time to add the corrective technique.

Once that happens…once your pup stops what he's doing when you say "No"…can you stop adding the corrective technique?

Well, unfortunately, if you stop adding an actual correction to "No" or if you add a correction only *sometimes*, some clever pups will go right back to repeating the behavior you were trying to stop. These pups have learned, you see, that your *No* sound doesn't **always** come with a negative consequence. So at any given time, they might choose to ignore the *No* sound, hoping that THIS could be one of those times when you're not going to enforce it.

Therefore, in the beginning when you're teaching *No*, you should try to pair it every time with an actual corrective technique.

 But once you've been working with your pup for a while and you have a great leader-follower relationship, usually you *can* just say "No." I can't remember the last time I had to use a corrective technique with any of my current dogs, because a simple "No" stops any behavior. In fact, they very seldom do any behavior that even requires a *No.* Something to look forward to!

Corrective techniques...what are they?

 A **leash tug** is the most common technique I use for stopping an undesirable behavior.

(1) Grasp the leash **6 to 18 inches** from your pup's collar. (2) Drop your hand to the **same height off the ground** as the collar. (3) Move your hand **toward** the collar to create a little slack in the leash. (4) Tug the leash **sideways** and **parallel** to the ground—a quick (one-second) tug that's just enough to make your pup stop the undesirable behavior. A young or sensitive puppy will need only a mild tug.

 A harmless **spray of water** from a plastic spray bottle or squirt gun. You want the pup to learn that "*this* behavior → *No* → wet."

However, a common mistake is to NAG a strong, determined pup with a bunch of tiny little tugs that he pays no attention to. Nagging is annoying to a dog. If ONE tug doesn't interrupt the pup's behavior and make it stop, the second one should be firmer, or else use a different kind of corrective technique.

A **sudden sharp noise.** The Barker Breaker® by the *Amtek Company* is a small handheld device that makes a shrill sound when you press the button. The sound startles many puppies, causing them to stop whatever they're doing (whether it's barking or something else). Just be forewarned that it's loud and shrill to human ears, too! A cheaper option is to put coins or nuts and bolts inside a metal can, tape the top shut, and shake the can.

 A *loud sound* correction is less useful when you have multiple dogs, because you don't want the one who is not misbehaving to feel corrected.

A **puff of compressed air.** The Pet Corrector® by *The Company of Animals* and The Pet Convincer® by *Canine Innovations* are small handheld devices that make a soft, startling hissing sound, which can interrupt bad behavior.

> Every pup is different. Some consider squirts of water to be great fun, but don't like noise. Others are unfazed by noise but dislike getting wet. You never know what will work for any particular pup.

Also, some corrective techniques work well for certain behaviors, but less well for other behaviors. As we go through the chapters in this book, I'll recommend effective techniques for common behaviors such as mouthing and nipping, barking, jumping on people, pulling on the leash, and so on.

Will corrections harm your relationship with your puppy?

Absolutely not. Corrections *strengthen* your relationship because the pup can see that *you* are making the rules about what he can and can't do. That reassures him that you've got the leadership position covered.

Then he can relax and be a good follower, which is much less stressful for a dog than trying to be a leader.

Does that mean puppies *enjoy* corrections? Of course not.

Puppies aren't going to act happy when you make them do something they don't want to do, or stop them from doing something they *want* to do. When things don't go his way, it's normal for a pup to flatten his ears, drop his tail, and "look sad."

I'm sure your kids have sulked when they weren't happy with one of your decisions. Heck, you and I did the same thing when we were kids! But we learned a valuable lesson about consequences and we quickly got over our pouting.

Establishing the proper leader-follower relationship that your puppy thrives on will ensure his ***long-term psychological health.*** All of us—adults, children, and dogs—make better decisions once we discover that there are indeed rules in life and that we are held accountable for our actions.

Chapter 6

Seven Mistakes to Avoid When Teaching "No"

At this point in the book, you've learned several ways to stop your puppy from doing something you don't want him to do.

We spend a lot of time on this because if you can immediately STOP bad behavior, you can control your pup in virtually any circumstance that crops up. So we want to get this right!

Let's look at seven common mistakes owners make when teaching "No."

1. Repeatedly saying "No" *without backing it up* with a corrective technique.

2. *Asking* (instead of telling) your puppy to stop what he's doing, or trying to "reason" with him.

3. Smiling or laughing when you say "No."

4. Petting or fondling your puppy while saying "No."

5. *Repeating the same corrective technique* even when it doesn't make your particular pup stop the behavior.

6. **Calling** your puppy when you're planning to correct him.

7. **Chasing** after him to correct him.

Let's look at those mistakes one at a time.

1) Don't say "No" without backing it up.

Jake story

When her TV show went to commercial, Kathy wandered into the kitchen for a glass of water. Through the window, she saw her dog Jake digging another hole in the tulip bed. She raised the window. "Jake, No! No!" Jake stopped digging and looked up. But Kathy was already hurrying back to the TV. Jake resumed his digging.

Here's what Jake learned from Kathy's "correction":

> That when he does certain things that he enjoys, his owner's head sometimes appears and vague sounds float out of her mouth. Nothing else happens.

Jake logically concludes that the sound *no* is an incidental background sound, no different from the incidental sounds of flying dirt he hears when he digs a hole.

The sound *no* carries no consequences. He can ignore it, just as he ignores the sound of the flying dirt. Just another one of life's little mysteries!

One of the most common mistakes owners make is to tell their puppy "No" and then allow him to continue the behavior. This simply confirms to him that *no* is a meaningless sound.

If you're ever in a position where you can't MAKE your pup stop a behavior (say you're at the top of a ladder with a bucket of paint and your puppy is barking), don't say "No" unless you're truly prepared to come down that ladder!

Be especially careful when you're occupied with something, such as talking on the phone. Some clever pups learn that if you're busy, you might yell, but you won't make them stop.

> Remember, your puppy is learning from you all the time. He can either learn good things or bad things from you. Your job is to make sure he only learns good things.

2) Don't ASK your puppy to stop what he's doing or try to "reason" with him.

Kathy held up her ruined sandal and waved it at her dog. "Jake, these sandals cost me 75 dollars and now you've ruined them. They were a perfect match for my turquoise outfit! It was wrong of you to do this, Jake. It was mean. You've made me very unhappy and you darned well better be sorry! Am I making myself clear, Jake? Do you understand me?"

Poor Jake. All he understands is that his owner is holding up a chew toy and spewing out a long monologue of harmless sounds. As she waves the sandal around, he stares longingly at it. He remembers where he got this tasty toy. He also remembers that there were lots more in the same place.

How you correct your puppy is important. Ranting, pleading, a barrage of words...those mean nothing to a dog. Just say "No" in a calm, confident, deep-ish voice and add a corrective technique.

3) Don't smile or laugh when you say "No."

Kathy's husband, Roger, couldn't help chuckling as he pulled their dog away from the spitting cat. "Hey, Jake, leave the cat alone, eh?" But he had to admit that it was amusing to see them bickering. Roger wasn't fond of the cat, anyway. As soon as he released Jake's collar, the dog charged after the cat again.

If you secretly think it's cute or funny when your puppy does something you don't want him to repeat, you need to keep those thoughts off your face and out of your voice.

Otherwise, your puppy will read your body language and conclude that your "No" isn't really serious.

> When you interact with your puppy, your tone of voice, facial expression, and body language are important. Work on your acting skills!

4) Don't add affection or petting to your corrections.

"Jake, how many times have I told you to stay off the sofa!" Kathy wrapped her arm around the dog and pushed him onto the floor. When he was off, she said "Good boy!" and tickled his head affectionately. As she headed for the kitchen, Jake jumped back onto the sofa.

A correction isn't much of a correction if it includes personal attention, touching, and praise. Make your corrections swift and impersonal, then turn your attention away from the pup for at least a few minutes. You want him to learn that only when he has been behaving well does he receive touching, petting, and praise.

5) Don't keep using a correction if it doesn't work for your puppy.

It's tempting to choose a particular corrective technique—for example, a harmless spray of water—because you like it. But the question should always be: *Does it work for your puppy?*

Roger was tired of Jake's incessant chewing. The sofa was pitted with holes like the craters on the moon. So he bought a plastic squirt gun, and when he caught Jake chewing, he ran toward the dog, squirting madly.

That was fine and dandy with Jake! He leaped happily into the air, trying to catch the water with his tongue. The "game" ended when Roger, backpedaling frantically, tripped over the ottoman and fell on his backside.

Later he returned to the living room and found Jake curled inside one of the holes in the sofa…chewing on the plastic squirt gun.

> This happens a lot. Owners will complain that they tried the spray of water or noisemaker or leash tug. And it didn't work.

Now, sometimes there is something amiss with their *timing.* They might not be quick enough to apply the corrective technique *in close enough proximity* to the behavior. For your puppy to understand the connection between the two, timing is important.

Or there might be something amiss with their *firmness.* They might be giving a big rowdy pup a single squirt of water or a half-hearted tug of the leash that would be better matched to a baby Chihuahua.

Or sometimes *consistency* is the problem. If you correct a behavior one day but allow it the next day, your puppy will never understand.

But sometimes a correction doesn't work simply because you've chosen the wrong correction for your particular pup.

> Your puppy will show you, by his body language, and especially by the *results,* whether a particular correction works for him. His tail will droop a bit or his ears flatten. His facial expression and body language will say, "Oops! Sorry about that!" Most importantly, he should stop the behavior immediately.

If he keeps right on doing what he's doing, or if he stops for a moment, then goes back to the misbehavior as soon as you turn your back, **you have not yet made the correction outweigh the reward he's getting from the behavior.**

You're looking for the corrective technique—and the *degree* of corrective technique—that **outweighs** the fun he is getting from the behavior. That's different for every pup and for every behavior.

Ultimately, then…

it is your PUP who decides which corrective technique you should use.

> Don't keep using a correction that doesn't work for your puppy. Increase its firmness, or adjust your timing, or try something else. A technique isn't "corrective" if it doesn't stop the problem.

6) Don't call your puppy if you're going to correct him.

If you call your pup and he comes to you, and then you scold him or do something he doesn't like (a bath, for example), he will associate the sound *Come* with unpleasantness and be reluctant to respond positively to that sound.

You don't want your puppy to think that obeying *Come* might cause discomfort.

And don't try to trick him by coaxing, "Come here, Jake. Mommy's not going to hurt you. Come on, sweetheart."

Because if your pup follows his trusting nature and believes you and then discovers your deception, he will not only distrust the word *Come* but also he might distrust YOU.

So whenever you need to correct your puppy or do anything uncomfortable with him, don't call him. Go get him. Silently.

And if your pup runs away from you when you're going to get him?

7) Don't chase your dog.

When the garbage can crashed to the kitchen floor, strewing trash everywhere, Jake knew he was in trouble. Kathy was rushing toward him, hands outstretched. Jake feinted left and rushed right. The chase was on!

When they don't want to be caught, many pups will dart just out of your reach and lead you on merry chases around the house.

You should never play this game. Every second that your puppy manages to elude you cheapens you in his eyes. He knows that followers shouldn't be able to defeat leaders.

Instead, track him down silently. Don't run. Walk firmly and purposefully. Don't say a word. Most pups are baffled and unnerved by such persistent, methodical following. In fact, many pups eventually shrink down and give up.

Let's assume your puppy has given up and/or you have cornered him so you can be sure of getting hold of his collar without any risk of lunging at him and missing. What should you do next?

Put a leash on him. See Chapter 11 for how to use a leash indoors (and outdoors, too, if he runs away from you outdoors). Some owners buy a cheap cotton leash and cut it short so it hangs down just short of the floor. This offers a decent handhold if you need to quickly get hold of the puppy.

As you progress through this book and establish your leader-follower relationship, he won't run away from you any more.

Chapter 7

All Family Members Should Be On the Same Page

I hear this all the time from clients: "Jake listens to me, but not to my wife."

Or vice versa.

In a multi-adult household, it often happens that one person projects the right attitude and says and does all the right things, while another person does not.

Accordingly, the puppy respects one person, but not the other.

If you're the only one working with the pup, the only one with the calm self-confident attitude, the only one following the program in this book *consistently,* your puppy will listen to you but not necessarily to your spouse and kids.

Dogs aren't robots that can be programmed to obey anyone who says the magic words. It's not the WORDS that cause a dog to listen to you and do what you want.

It's the proper leader-follower relationship that causes a dog to listen and do what you want.

> It's important for ALL of the adults in the household to build the right leader-follower relationship with the puppy.

Your dog wants black-and-white rules and routines.

Suppose you and your spouse allow different behaviors. **You** chase the puppy off the sofa but pat your waist to invite him to jump on you. Your **spouse** lets the puppy stay on the sofa but scolds him for jumping on her.

There might even be a third family member, or a housekeeper, or even the folks at doggy daycare, who won't correct the puppy for anything.

The Rules

These inconsistencies need to stop. At least during the first year or two that you're working with your puppy, there should be no "maybes" or "sometimes."

You may think you're being nice by being "flexible" about what your pup is allowed to do.

Your puppy, on the other hand, pegs you as **indecisive.** Now he feels anxious, uncertain, and compelled to second-guess your decisions and test your rules to find out which ones are real and which ones are up for grabs.

Dogs feel most secure when their world is "always this" and "always that." Consistent, predictable, black-and-white. Dogs do not do well with *gray* areas.

> So if mixed messages are happening in your pup's life, sort it out quickly. Either get everyone on board with your training program or keep your puppy away from people who are (even unintentionally) undermining it. Your pup will appreciate that!

Chapter 8

Teaching "Yes"

We've been focusing on handling undesirable behavior, but we mustn't take **good** behavior for granted.

Good behavior is much more likely to be repeated if you let your pup know that you like it.

Think of how pleased you feel when your spouse says, "That was a great dinner, hon" or "Thanks for raking the lawn—it looks so nice." Or when your boss says, "Good job on that report."

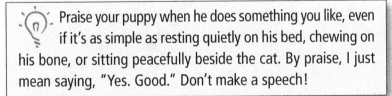

Praise your puppy when he does something you like, even if it's as simple as resting quietly on his bed, chewing on his bone, or sitting peacefully beside the cat. By praise, I just mean saying, "Yes. Good." Don't make a speech!

The energy level of your voice matters

When you want *activity* from your pup, use an *animated* voice.

Suppose he's across the yard. You call him and when he starts toward you, praise him. Now, if you just said "Good dog" in a bored tone, that's not very motivating, is it? But he might break into an enthusiastic run if you call happily, "Yes! **GOOD** boy! Yay!"

When you want *calmness* from your pup, use a *calm* voice.

Suppose he's resting on his bed. If you burst into "Yay! What a good dog you are!", your nice relaxed puppy might leap up and begin cavorting around the room. That's counterproductive. When he should be calm and he *is* being calm, be *quietly* approving: "Gooood boy. Good."

Some scenarios call for both calmness and animation. During a potty break, as your puppy squats to pee, give a word of approval in a low-key voice. You don't want him excited or distracted.

But when he's completely done peeing and pooping, then you can exclaim, "Yes! Good boy! You did it!" in your animated voice, accompanied by a treat and then a minute or two of fun play.

Are treats necessary to train a dog?

No. As your puppy tries different behaviors throughout the day, your job is simply to give a thumbs-up or a thumbs-down.

Many pups are perfectly content for your thumbs-up to be a word of approval, a rub of his ears, an affectionate tickle under his chin, a scratch of his chest, a gentle thump of his shoulder, or a toss of his favorite toy.

And yet…most pups do learn more quickly and eagerly when you use food. But to avoid *relying* on food, you need to progress from **constant** treating (every time) to **variable** treating (every other time, or every third time) to **random** treating (only occasionally).

When you *shouldn't* use food

- **Don't use food** when your pup is doing a behavior you don't like, or has just finished doing a behavior you don't like. If your puppy is (or has just been) nipping at your hands or jumping on you or barking, don't give him a treat. Dogs look for patterns and they *repeat* behaviors that result in food.

- **Don't use food** when your pup is acting afraid of something. No, the food won't "reassure" him. Instead, it *reinforces* his fearful behavior and you'll see more fear, not less.

- **Don't use food** if your puppy gets over-excited. Some pups, when they see food, will jump and whine and turn off their brain. With these pups, use treats minimally, if at all.

- **Don't use food** as a bribe. A bribe is when you show the puppy a treat and then give him a command. Many pups are happy to obey "Sit" as long as you're waving a treat. If they don't see the treat, they say, "Pfft…why should I?" Now, when you're first teaching certain words, you *can* use a treat to "lure" your puppy into the right position. But once he understands, you want to phase out the treats.

Once your puppy understands a command, you shouldn't let him see any food before he has obeyed that command. In other words, say "Sit" **but don't even move your hand toward your pocket** where the treats are. *After* the pup sits, say, "Yes" or "Good." **Then** reach into your pocket for the treat.

Say the word. Pup does the behavior. Praise. Reach for the treat. That way, you're not bribing the puppy and you can easily phase out the treats.

What kind of food rewards should you use?

Some people use dry kibble. They measure out what the puppy would have eaten that day and instead of feeding it in regular meals, they dole it out one kibble at a time all through the day, whenever the pup does a desirable behavior.

Using kibble can certainly work. But I don't do it because...

- First, I don't recommend feeding kibble to dogs. Read the feeding recommendations in my canine health care book, *11 Things You Must Do Right To Keep Your Dog Healthy and Happy.*

- Second, kibble takes too long to chew. Often the puppy ends up dribbling pieces onto the floor, then snuffles around for the crumbs rather than paying attention to me. I prefer food rewards to be soft so the pup can swallow them quickly.

> I also like treats to be tiny. Then the puppy can enjoy lots of rewards for good behavior, without getting fat or too full for his regular meals. Boiled or baked chicken works great for most pups—tiny pieces about ¼ to ½ the size of your thumbnail.

I put a handful of treats in a sandwich-size plastic baggie, then tuck the bag into my front pocket so the mouth of the bag is somewhat open to quickly reach in and grab a treat.

Food shouldn't be your only reward

Don't be so eager to pop a treat into your puppy's mouth that you forget about the more personal rewards you can offer.

Instead of a treat, you can fondle your pup's ears…scratch his chest… gently thump his shoulder…or give a quick tickle under his chin.

And don't forget the verbal praise! These "old-fashioned" rewards are time-honored ways to express approval and appreciation to your puppy.

But just as there are some puppies who get over-excited about food, some puppies get over-stimulated by petting and will start jumping around and nudging for more. If petting distracts your pup from paying attention, keep your hands off him so he can focus on the lesson.

If your puppy is difficult to motivate

Some pups are not interested in treats, although often this is just a matter of trying different **kinds.** Some pups dislike commercial treats but are happy to take bits of cooked chicken.

If your puppy loves to play or chase things, he might prefer the promise of a toy or game instead of food.

> For example, you call your puppy from across the yard and he comes galloping to you, whereupon you toss his favorite toy for him to play with.

If your puppy isn't motivated by either treats or toys, don't despair. Dogs have been trained for centuries without using either. My first few dogs were among the happiest and best-behaved dogs I've ever had and I used neither treats nor toys for their training.

> So if you don't want to use food, or if your puppy isn't motivated by it, just use verbal praise and physical touch. And if he isn't motivated by praise or touch either? Then I won't lie to you: training is going to be a challenge!

Chapter 9

Calmness Indoors is Essential

Calmness—both physical and mental calmness—is the foundation for all training. It's harder to get good behavior from a puppy who is excitable and reactive. By *excitable* and *reactive*, I mean a pup who is easily aroused, quick to respond to whatever he sees or hears, and doesn't relax unless he's asleep.

For example, an excitable or reactive puppy:

- runs around the house

- plays roughly with your other pet(s), wrestling and chasing

- barks when he hears the neighbor's dog bark

- leaps on and off the furniture

- barks out the window at people or other dogs

- jumps on people

- barks at the TV

- runs away from you when you try to get hold of him

- barks at the vacuum cleaner

- runs through doors ahead of you

- goes cuckoo when you get the leash to go for a walk, or when you get his food bowl out of the cupboard

- makes so much noise when someone knocks at the door that you find yourself trying to read the person's lips at the same time you're trying to grab hold of the puppy

Why are some dogs calmer and some dogs more excitable?

Age is a factor—young dogs tend to be more excitable than seniors. **Heredity** is also a factor—some breeds tend to be more excitable than others.

> But excitability is also a *learned* behavior that has been (unintentionally) encouraged and rewarded by the owner.

For example, you pick up the leash and your puppy barks and leaps with joy. You struggle to attach it as he squirms and wriggles. It's hard to open the door when he's jumping against it. Finally it opens and he surges past you. He spies another dog on the sidewalk and lunges forward, barking, his toenails scrabbling on the porch. Time for another "peaceful" walk! (In Chapters 11–12, you'll learn how to fix these issues.)

Remember, dogs learn from patterns. If your pup goes crazy and you follow that up with a walk, here is the pattern you're teaching: "Go crazy → go for a walk". Excitability should not be rewarded.

Calmness starts with *YOU*

From your dog's viewpoint, the leader sets the emotional tone for the family group. Interact with your puppy in a calm, deliberate manner. Don't rush around, gesture wildly, shout, or grab at him.

Be aware of your body language. Your puppy expects a leader to project calm confidence. When you deliver that, the pup feels satisfied that he had you "pegged" right. That makes him feel more settled and relaxed.

Calm handling can transform an excitable puppy.

When I meet a new client, I stand back and observe as their pup pulls on the leash, barks at whatever, jumps on the owner, pretty much hyped-up and out of control.

Then I approach. As I talk with the owner in a relaxed voice, I reach over and take the leash. I don't speak to the puppy or even look at him. I just keep talking to the owner, and occasionally I give a leash correction when the pup jumps around with excitability or barks.

Within a minute or two, the pup stops jumping, stops pulling, stops barking. A minute more, and he's standing or sitting quietly.

Same puppy.

An excited dog can often be transformed into a more relaxed dog in a matter of minutes, using only confident body language and proper leash communication. Yes, you can use the leash to carry on a conversation with your pup.

The first step to indoor calmness and good behavior

Over the course of this book, I'm going to show you how to stop excitable and reactive behavior issues such as barking, rushing the doorbell, jumping on people, pulling on the leash, and dashing through doors ahead of you.

 The *FIRST* step to indoor calmness and better behavior is to control your puppy's movements in the house.

The biggest mistake owners make with a puppy is giving him too much freedom, too soon.

Being loose in the house should be a *privilege* that is s-l-o-w-ly earned—*after* the puppy matures, is 100% housebroken, is calm and quiet, has learned all the rules and routines of your household, and has no behavior issues.

There's no reason that a puppy needs to be wandering around the house. That simply gives him more opportunities to practice undesirable behaviors. Pups who practice undesirable behaviors end up with bad *habits.*

I limit a puppy's movements indoors until:

 he has been in my household for at least 3 months AND he is at least 10 months old AND 100% housebroken (no accidents for months) AND follows all of the routines of my household.

When a dog meets those criteria, I start letting him wander around a few rooms *when I'm home.* When he reaches 18–24 months old, I start testing to see if he can be free in the house *when I'm gone.*

> You might think that's a long time to wait. But your pup is going to be with you for 10 to 15 years. Surely you can afford to be ultravigilant for just 1 to 2 of those years, thereby ensuring that all the remaining years will be problem-free.

How to control your puppy's movements indoors

✓ If he is not 100% housebroken, he should be in a crate (Chapter 13) or wire pen (Chapter 14) whenever you're not interacting with him.

✓ If he is 100% house-broken, he should be restricted (with portable baby gates) to the same room you're in. Or keep him on a leash so he must follow you around the house as you do chores, or hang out with you when you watch TV or read a book or answer your email. All of which encourages calmness and the right leader-follower relationship.

> A puppy with a leash on should be supervised at all times so he can't get the leash tangled around anything. **Never leave a dog alone with a leash on!**

What your pup should do when he's on leash indoors

If you're walking around, he should follow you without pulling on the leash. If you're sitting down, toss a dog bed on the floor near your feet. Put a safe chew toy like a Nylabone® or Kong® toy on the bed.

Your puppy can choose to:

 lie down on the bed or floor

 chew on the toy

 wander around within the length of the 6-foot leash

 or just stand there looking around

Praise good behavior. If he is doing any of the above, give him a quiet, approving "Good boy."

Avoid touching and eye contact. Puppies find it harder to relax if you're touching them or looking at them. Be aware of what your pup is doing, but don't stare at him.

Correct any behavior you don't want repeated:

- Pulling on the leash (Chapter 11)

- Barking (Chapter 24)

- Jumping on you or anyone else (Chapter 25)

> Your job is to set consistent boundaries. "Yes" to this. "No" to that. When your puppy sees you doing that, he recognizes that you are the trusted leader and he is the trusting follower.

Chapter 10

Introducing a Young Puppy to the Leash

This chapter is for pups who have never had a leash on, or who won't walk when you put their leash on. If your pup already walks confidently on a leash (even if he pulls you around), you can skip this chapter and go on to Chapter 11.

New pups who have never had a leash on

Put on a buckle collar. Let the puppy wear it for a day to get used to it. He might scratch at it, but that will pass.

Attach a lightweight leash, 4- to 6-feet, with a lightweight snap.

Let your puppy lead you at first. Put no pressure on the leash. Just follow him around so he gets used to the two of you moving in close proximity.

Time to stand still! Now…holding your end of the leash, stand still. It shouldn't take long before your puppy, wandering around, tightens the leash so it's pulling on his collar. If he doesn't wander away on his own, take a few steps in any direction, just enough that the leash gets taut. Then stand still.

Now observe what happens:

 Some pups feel the pressure on their collar and quickly discover that if they move toward you, the pressure stops. Praise the pup "Yes! Good!" and reward with a treat. Repeat lots of times. **You're teaching the puppy the valuable lesson of "yielding" to leash pressure.**

 Some pups don't seem to notice (or mind) the pressure on their collar. They're so eager to run around that they pull happily in all directions. That's okay for now! We'll get the pulling under control in the next chapter.

 Some pups become ***vigorously resistant*** when they feel pressure on their collar. They spin around to face you, rear up on their hind legs, leap around like a hooked fish, bite the leash, wrap their front feet over the leash, even yelp.

 Finally, some pups are ***passively resistant.*** They stand facing you at the end of the leash, feet braced, head turned to one side, refusing to move.

> Whether your pup is ***vigorously*** or ***passively*** resistant, **DON'T** respond with sympathetic murmurings. **DON'T** pull the pup toward you, but also **DON'T** release the tension on the leash. Just hold your end calmly, as though *you* don't see any problem here.

If the pup doesn't quickly figure out how to relieve the pressure by moving in your direction, crouch down and pat your leg to encourage him to come toward you. You want him to learn that **HE** has the power to stop the pressure by moving toward you.

When he finally takes even one step toward you, praise with your animated voice ("Yes! Good puppy!") and hold out a treat. That should get his attention and hopefully get him trotting the rest of the way to you so you can give him the treat.

Pups who really won't walk

A few pups are determined that they're not going to walk at all. Some will even sit or lie down.

1) Start with treats!

Hold a tiny piece of boiled or baked chicken in front of his nose. When he leans toward it, make him walk a step or two before giving it to him. Praise!

Gradually make him take more steps before you will give the treat. Three steps…treat. Five steps…treat. Seven steps…treat. He needs to work for his food!

To save yourself a spot of back pain from bending way down with a treat, get a long wooden spoon from your kitchen. Smear some peanut butter and cheese on it. Hold the spoon in front of the pup's nose and see if he will trot beside you, occasionally getting a lick of the spoon.

> The problem is that some clever pups decide they won't walk unless they see a treat. And you can't bribe them forever.

2) Use *alternating pressure* on the leash.

If you have a very stubborn pup, just start walking. If the pup doesn't move, the leash will obviously become taut when you reach the end. Don't stop walking. Move your hand quickly *toward* the pup, which will create a bit of slack in the leash.

That will catch him by surprise. He might even wobble a bit since there is no longer a tight leash to brace against. Take advantage of his surprise by quickly pulling him toward you **just enough to make him take a couple of steps.**

Remember to keep walking as you do this, and keep encouraging him to follow you. Every time the pup refuses to walk, or sits or lies down, use that alternating technique (loosen/tighten/loosen) that should make him take a couple of steps.

> Walk, walk, walk…that's the key to getting a balky pup to start moving. He's attached to the leash, so if you keep moving, he *has* to move also.

By alternately loosening, tightening, and loosening the leash, as you keep walking slowly, you'll be able to move the pup in the same direction you're walking, a few steps at a time. Yes, it will be a bit *herky-jerky* for him, but that won't last long.

Remember, dogs are opportunists. They want to do things that bring them some benefit and to avoid doing things that cause discomfort. Your pup will discover that he can stop the *herky-jerky* movement and walk comfortably if he simply trots along with you.

Now on to real leash training!

Chapter 11

Walk Nicely on the Leash

A puppy who is pulling on the leash is focused on himself and his environment—sights, sounds, smells, other people, other dogs—that is, everything in his environment *except* his owner.

Often the pup doesn't even notice you at the other end of the leash. This oblivious attitude is not respectful.

So if your pup is at least 10 weeks old, we're going to give him a job to do. We're going to teach him that it's **his** responsibility to keep the leash loose. When his leash is on, his job is to pay attention to your whereabouts and stay close enough to you that the leash is always loose—whether you're sitting, standing, or walking around.

This simple job helps your puppy become an attentive, respectful follower.

> If you've had trouble taking your pup for walks in the past, I recommend that you NOT take him for any walks right now.

Instead, work with him in your house and yard until he is nearly flawless on the leash. Then you can add distractions by taking him out in public.

Follow these four steps to teach your puppy to respect the leash and not pull:

1. First, learn the *Loosen-Tug* technique—the key to leash control

2. For strong pullers, consider alternative collars

3. Play the *Sneak Away* game—don't skip this one!

4. Play the *Opposite Direction* game—again, very important!

Let's make sure your dog has the right collar and leash

For most pups, start with a flat buckle collar of nylon or leather. It simply buckles around your puppy's neck. Some pups never need anything more.

For toy breed puppies, you can try a lightweight collar, but some toys have a delicate windpipe and a collar makes them cough. If that happens, you can switch to a harness. I like a soft mesh harness like the Puppia® brand (pictured).

> Pups who are larger, or who are very strong pullers, might need a different kind of collar. We'll find out in just a few minutes.

Leashes

I recommend a 4-foot to 6-foot leash that is 3/8" to 1/2" wide, and soft and comfortable in your hands. Some nylon leashes feel too sharp. Well-worn leather is great, but new leather is very stiff.

There will be times when you'll want a longer leash so you can move farther away from your puppy, but still maintain control. A 15- to 20-foot leash or strong cord works well.

Step #1: Learn the Loosen-Tug technique

This might sound like an odd question...but do you have a stuffed animal in your house? A plush teddy bear, for example, or some other lightweight object that's roughly the size of your puppy.

Why? Because I'm going to explain some leash-handling techniques and you might want to hook your leash to a stuffed toy so you can practice before you try them with your puppy. Then you'll feel more confident that you know exactly what to do.

> So I'm going to explain the steps using the word *puppy,* but I do hope you might practice them first with the stuffed animal.

Go stand somewhere in your house or yard. Use the leash to maneuver your (puppy) so he's standing close to you, no farther than a foot or so away. It doesn't matter whether he's in front of you or on either side of you, as long as he's within a foot or so.

Look at the clip of the leash. Is it hanging straight down below his neck? If you're holding him with a tight leash, the clip can't be hanging straight down. So "pay out" (loosen) some of the leash until the clip is hanging under his neck and pointing down at the ground.

The section of leash that's attached to the clip should be forming a little U-shape before it starts climbing up into your hand.

 That's where you want your puppy to be. Everything you do now should be focused on getting your pup to stay within a foot or two of you, with the clip hanging down and the leash loose.

Don't walk anywhere. Just stand there. If your puppy just stands there too, tell him quietly that he's a good boy. You want him to be calm, so use a calm voice.

If instead your puppy moves away from you so the leash gets tight, you're going to do the *Loosen-Tug* technique:

 Reach down with one hand and grasp the leash about 12 to 18 inches from your pup's collar. Lower that hand down to the **same height off the ground** as the collar. Your hand doesn't need to be NEAR the collar—just the *same height off the ground*.

 Move that hand quickly **toward** your puppy. That will create a tiny bit of slack in the leash. This is the **loosen** part of the *Loosen-Tug* technique.

Then move that hand quickly **away** from your puppy, keeping your hand **parallel to the ground** as you pull your pup back to within a foot or so of your leg. Either leg.

Immediately loosen the leash so the clip is hanging down and that lovely U-shape reappears in the leash.

> Don't **HOLD** your puppy close to you. Pull him close, then immediately loosen the leash. Clip hanging straight down? Check. U-shape in the leash? Check. Don't **HOLD** your dog close to you.

This lesson is all about repetition. Keep giving your pup the opportunity to move away from you by loosening the leash.

If he takes advantage of the opportunity and moves away from you, drop your hand down to his collar height, then hand-forward (create slack), hand-backward and *parallel to the ground,* and pull him back. Then loosen the leash again.

Remain calm. You want your puppy to be calm, so keep your own movements calm. Correct him methodically. Don't say anything. Whenever he stops pulling and stands there on a loose leash, give him a single quiet "Yes. Good boy." Don't get him revved-up.

If your puppy is still pulling

With persistent pups, change the gentle ***pull*** into more of a ***tug,*** which is quicker and a little more jarring.

Drop your hand to collar height. Hand forward—create slack. Hand backward—parallel to the ground—in a fast "popping" ***tug*** that gets your determined pup's attention as you pull him closer to you. Then loosen the leash. Hopefully your pup will decide that pulling on the leash isn't worth that *tug.*

But if he keeps pulling hard, it's time to try a different collar.

Although a regular buckle collar **looks** mild, it exerts force on one concentrated point on your pup's throat if he's a hard puller.

That puts a lot of pressure on his throat, so you'll need to stop the pulling with a safer training tool.

Step #2: Alternative collars (listed in no particular order)

Martingale collar

A martingale collar tightens **evenly** around your pup's neck if he pulls. So the pressure is distributed around the neck instead of being concentrated on one point on the throat. A properly fitting martingale can only tighten to a certain point and no farther. It can't "choke" your puppy. *PetSafe* is a popular brand.

British slip collar

This is a combination of collar and leash all in one. This collar should be kept HIGH on a strong pup's neck, right behind his ears. A good brand is *Mendota*.

Fig. F-1

Head halter

You've probably seen horses being led around with a rope attached to a halter. The theory is that where the head goes, the rest of the body follows. Two popular head halters for dogs are *Gentle Leader* (pictured) and *Halti*.

A head halter can turn some hyperactive pullers into calm followers with very little effort. Other pups fight the unfamiliar pressure on their face and become panicky, though often this reaction is short-lived and then the puppy settles down.

Front-attachment harness

This is NOT a regular harness. With a regular harness, you clip the leash to a ring on the dog's **back.**

A regular harness is designed to help sled dogs *pull,* so if you put a regular harness on a puppy who is already a puller, you're just making it easier for him to pull. Not what you want!

But a *front-attachment* harness can be effective. Here you clip the leash onto a ring on the puppy's **chest.**

If he lunges forward and hits the end of the leash, he gets turned around in a little semi-circle until he's facing YOU instead of what he was pulling toward.

Some front-attachment harnesses I recommend include:

 Petsafe Easy Walk Harness (pictured)

 Freedom No-Pull Harness

 Kurgo Tru-Fit Smart Harness

 Sense-ation No-Pull Harness

They're each a little different in design, so you'll need to test them to see which, if any, might work with your puppy.

Herm Sprenger prong collar

If your pup is at least six months old and is a powerful puller, you might try a *HERM SPRENGER* prong collar. I don't recommend other brands.

A prong collar distributes pressure around your pup's neck *evenly,* so it's safer than a buckle collar, which concentrates its pressure on the front of the throat. A prong collar can only close so far—it can't choke your pup.

If you're worried about those prongs, you needn't be. On the *Herm Sprenger* brand that I recommend, the prongs are rounded and blunt. They can't "stab" your pup. What they do is close together in a light "pinching" action of the loose skin on his neck…

…IF he pulls.

If he just walks beside you, there is no more pressure on his neck than if he was wearing a regular buckle collar. So he's the one who decides whether to pull and get pinched, or not.

A *Herm Sprenger* prong collar is like the *power steering* on your car, in which the smallest movement of the steering wheel makes the car respond. With a prong collar, you need to give only a **very gentle** tug (just a twitch of your wrist) and most pups respond instantly by stopping their pulling.

Cautions about alternative collars

First, these are *training* tools. Don't leave them on your pup when no one is watching him. He could get them caught on something.

Second, these tools should be used on a **temporary** basis, to get across to the puppy that you want him to stand and walk quietly on a loose leash.

If your puppy is only controllable when he's wearing a specialty training tool, he's respecting the **tool**—not you. That's fine at first, but your goal is to establish the right leader-follower relationship in which your pup stays beside you simply because of **YOU.**

> A trusting follower dog has so much respect for you, so much faith in you as a leader, that he *wants* to be close to you.

Step #3: Play the Sneak-Away game

Once your puppy will stand beside you on a loose leash, once he clearly understands that he mustn't pull when you're standing still… it's time for you to move.

Take three steps. Then stop. Where is your pup?

 Did he follow you so that the leash is still loose? "Yes! Good!"

 Or did he move away so the leash is now tight? Use the *Loosen-Tug technique*—hand forward to create slack, hand backward to move him a foot or so in your direction, so the leash becomes loose again.

> Remember, you don't want to hold him on a tight leash. It's going to be *HIS* job to keep the leash loose by paying attention to your whereabouts and following you. When he isn't doing his job, your job is to remind him to do it.

Take another three (or more) steps and stop. Your steps can be forward, to the left, to the right, even backward. Make it a game in which you try to sneak away from your puppy when he isn't paying attention. Don't forget the praise if he *is* being attentive!

Most pups end up loving this game and are quite pleased with themselves when you can no longer sneak away from them!

When your puppy becomes good enough at this game that no matter what direction you go in, he follows you and the leash always remains loose, it's time to...

Step #4: Play the Opposite-Direction game

Maneuver your pup onto your left or right side. He should be within about 12 inches of your leg, with his head roughly *even* with your leg (a little bit behind or ahead of your leg is fine).

Whichever side your puppy is on, hold the leash in that hand. Drop that arm so it's hanging down beside you, the way you would normally walk. Is the clip of the leash hanging straight down? Is there a nice U-shape where the leash comes off the clip and starts climbing up into your hand? That's the lovely loose leash we're looking for!

When he's walking nicely, praise him and give an occasional tiny treat if you like—but don't stop walking!

> Whenever the leash doesn't look like that, or whenever your pup gets half of his body ahead of your leg or too far off to the side, it's your job to bring him back into position.

Along with the **Loosen-Tug** technique, there's a little game called **Opposite-Direction** that will quickly get your puppy sticking more closely to your leg.

Here's the game—when he forges ahead, turn and walk briskly in the opposite direction. You can reverse direction by turning *away* from your pup, or by turning *toward* your pup.

I'll explain how to do it both ways.

Reverse direction by turning AWAY from your puppy.

Suppose he's walking on your left side. Make a **180-degree turn to your right.** For you military marchers out there, that's a "right about-turn."

Keep walking the whole time. Now your puppy will find himself behind you and will need to hurry to catch up.

If he catches up but charges past you, reverse yourself again. Again he will find himself trailing behind and will need to scramble to catch up.

It won't be long before he realizes that for some bizarre reason, *whenever he forges ahead,* it causes you to walk in the opposite direction.

You should start to see him be reluctant to move ahead of you, lest he cause one of your cuckoo direction changes.

> Good! Your pup should not be in front of you where he can't even see you. He should walk *beside* you, using his eyeballs to keep tabs on your whereabouts. It's the respectful thing to do.

Reverse direction by turning TOWARD your puppy.

This turn, where you make a **180-degree turn to your left,** is a little more complicated because the pup is in your way. You don't want to trip over him.

Turn left toward your pup *before* he has gotten ahead of your leg. You can even use the leash to hold him back behind you a bit as you begin to make the turn.

Assuming he's on your left side, pivot on your left foot and AS you make the turn, swing your RIGHT leg/foot in an exaggerated motion across your body and in front of your puppy's head. Your swinging leg/foot will remind him to hang back as you complete the 180-degree turn and walk in the opposite direction.

> If you make frequent about-turns (to the right and to the left), pulling can be stopped quickly. **If it isn't working for your pup, revisit the earlier section on alternative collars.**

Pups who won't walk

Some puppies are determined not to walk at all. See Chapter 10 for what to do with these pups.

Chapter 12

Go for a Structured Walk

A structured walk is a leadership-building experience between you and your pup (I recommend that he be at least 4 months old).

It's deceptively simple. Your pup simply walks beside you. Left side or right side doesn't matter, but once you've chosen a side, that's the side he should stay on (for that particular walk).

 He doesn't pull on the leash.

 He doesn't drop his head to sniff at the ground.

 He doesn't stop to go to the bathroom. Before the walk, he should have a chance to relieve himself in your yard.

> This is not a potty break or sightseeing tour. Your pup is going on a walk with *YOU* and he should pay attention to *YOU*.

Don't worry, there will be times during the walk when he **can** sniff around and eliminate.

You'll give him that freedom when you come to a good spot for those activities. Once we start the structured walk, you'll see how that works.

But first, is your pup *ready* for a structured walk?

 If you attach his leash, then just stand still, does he keep the leash loose? In other words, does he hover close enough to you that the leash doesn't get tight?

 If you sit in a chair while he's on leash, does he still keep the leash loose?

 If you stand up and walk in any direction, does he still keep the leash loose?

To go on a structured walk, your pup needs to be able to do *loose leash walking* (Chapter 11).

If your pup is fine on the leash, great job! He might be ready for a structured walk. But there's one other test...

 Does he sit politely (no barking, no jumping) while you attach his leash?

 When you open the door to go outside, does he wait for your permission before going through the door?

If yes to both questions, your pup is ready to do a structured walk with you.

You might be wondering why those last two questions are important. What does sitting politely and waiting for permission to go through a door have to do with going for a walk?

Only everything!

The most important part of the structured walk is BEFORE you start to walk. **In other words, the structured walk actually begins INSIDE your house.**

If you have trouble getting your pup to stay still while you attach the leash…if he jumps on you…if he barks and won't stop when you tell him to…if he tries to forge through the door when you open it…he isn't ready for a structured walk.

His body isn't calm. His state of mind isn't calm. A pup with an excited body and mind *indoors* will have the same excited body and mind *outdoors*.

These are the pups who pull on the leash, bark at other dogs, jump on people, and get distracted by everything they see and hear, instead of paying attention to *YOU*.

If your pup is out of control *before* the walk, it will be much harder to get him under control *during* the walk.

So you should get those behaviors under control before you try a structured walk. *Wait* at the door is in Chapter 15. Barking is in Chapter 24. Jumping is in Chapter 25.

Let's be optimistic and assume that your pup passed the tests, you've given him the "Okay" to go through the door, and you're both ready for a structured walk!

Once you get outside with your *calm* pup, give the signal for a structured walk.

After you've done all the teaching you need to do to get your pup calm and respectful indoors **before** the walk, give him permission to go through the door, "Okay."

Outside, have him *Sit* beside you. If he doesn't know *Sit* yet (Chapter 31), use a little upward pressure on the leash and downward pressure on his hindquarters to guide him into a *Sit*.

Then say, "Jake, heel" (or "Jake, close").

Which word to use? If you might do obedience competition with your pup in the future, use "Close" (as in "Stay close"). "Heel" is typically used in competitive canine events to mean a more precise type of walking that we don't cover in this book. If competition isn't your thing, pick either word.

"Sit" and then "Heel" (or "Close") will be the signals to your pup that you're going on a structured walk.

During the structured walk

First and foremost, you and your pup should be *together*. He shouldn't be pulling or walking ahead of you, looking at everything but you. The relationship you want to build is one in which you are the leader and your pup is the follower.

If he tries to forge ahead, don't forget the *Opposite-Direction* technique! It's one of the best ways to teach a dog to stay close.

Besides staying pretty close to your leg, your pup should keep his head up. No sniffing the ground, which is just one step removed from eating things off the ground. Stay alert. Scan the ground ahead for bits of trash and be ready to correct sniffing.

Your pup shouldn't be looking for places to eliminate. Dogs who want to pee against every vertical object often become obsessed with "marking territory" (Chapter 42).

Try to choose a route that doesn't offer tempting places to eliminate. Or walk in the street, if it's safe. If your pup suddenly eliminates anyway…oh well.

Your puppy should walk quietly. He shouldn't bark or lunge at passersby or other dogs (Chapters 43–44).

Break time!

Plan a route that includes a safe "potty break" place. Here you can say the magic release word: "Okay!"

This means your pup is free to romp about a bit, sniff the ground, find a place to pee, etc. If the area is large enough, you might be able to replace the leash with a 15- to 30-foot leash or cord so the puppy has more space to stretch his legs.

Bring along a ball or toy so you can interact with your pup. Make yourself interesting, make yourself a source of fun and play, as well as a source of guidance and direction. Then your pup will gravitate to you as someone he both trusts and enjoys being with.

The break needn't be very long. Five or ten minutes is fine. Then get your pup sitting beside you with a loose leash. Say, "Heel" or "Close" and continue with the structured walk back to your house.

You might be wondering, "Can I sometimes take my puppy for a *non*-structured walk? Where he can wander around on the leash, sniff the ground, and pee when he wants to?"

My answer is "Maybe." It depends on your pup.

- If he is over 4 months old, he should definitely learn how to do a structured walk. But if he is already well-behaved and doesn't pull on the leash, it's fine to do non-structured walks, as well.

- And if you have an older pup or adolescent dog with any behavior issues, **structured walks are a must for developing your leader-follower relationship.** Until those behavior issues stop, a structured walk is the *only* kind of walk you should take with that particular pup.

 For non-structured walks, I just say, "Let's go." But I still don't allow any pulling.

Chapter 13

Go into Your Crate and Stay Quietly

Every puppy should have a crate. Absolutely, positively, every pup should be taught how to stay quietly in a crate.

Eight reasons your puppy needs a crate:

1) A crate teaches calmness and relaxation.

Teaching your puppy to stay quietly in his crate is a perfect lesson in patience and impulse control. He learns that he must do some things simply because you want him to. This furthers your leader-follower relationship and makes the pup feel more secure.

When I hear an owner declare "My dog hates his crate!", I first check to make sure the pup is not being crated for 6+ hours a day while the owners go to work and the kids to school.

But if that's not the case and the dog still "hates" his crate, it's usually because the dog is excitable, reactive, anxious, or dependent. Hating the crate is just a symptom of those underlying problems.

> The good news is that learning to stay in a crate will *solve* some of those issues. When an excitable, reactive, anxious, or dependent dog learns to relax and be calm in a crate, it's much easier to teach him to relax and be calm in the house and on the leash. Crate-training is a valuable lesson that carries over to other behavior issues.

2) A crate makes housebreaking easier.

Most pups have an instinct to keep their sleeping quarters clean. As long as you take them outside frequently enough (every 2 to 4 hours during the day), they will try to not eliminate in the crate. See Chapter 34 on housebreaking.

3) A crate prevents destructive chewing, keeps your belongings safe, and keeps the *puppy* safe.

Destructive chewers can do massive damage to your home, plus they risk swallowing something that could choke or poison them. Veterinary emergency rooms are filled with dogs undergoing surgery for blocked intestines.

4) A crate keeps your puppy safe in the car.

You and your children are buckled in, right? Your pup should be, too. My dogs travel in a crate that is buckled into the backseat. Or you can buy a special car harness for dogs which attaches him to the seat belt in the backseat.

5) A crate is the perfect nighttime bed.

When your pup is sleeping safely in his crate, you don't have to worry about what else he might be doing all night.

6) All dogs should be accustomed to a crate so they won't be stressed at the vet's or groomer's office.

A pup who is accustomed to a crate will be much less stressed when he has to stay temporarily in one at the vet. As our dog's guardian, *it's our responsibility to prepare him for the real world* so he's not frightened by normal things that might happen to him.

7) A crate confines your pup for short "emergency" periods.

For example, when you have guests over who are allergic to (or uncomfortable around) dogs. When your dog has had surgery and the vet recommends *crate rest* for a few days.

There will be plenty of times when you need your pup to be safely confined. Then you'll be very glad you have a crate on hand and that your dog has been taught how to be calm and quiet in it!

8) A crate provides a safe and secure sanctuary.

Your dog can nap or sit and observe the world from the refuge of his den. Once he has freedom of the house, you can leave the crate door open and he will go into the crate on his own and sleep. My adult dogs go in and out of their crates freely.

How long can a dog stay in a crate?

During the day, **a dog should be in a crate for no more than 2–3 hours at a time,** after which he should get a potty break, a brief activity session, and a drink of water.

 Therefore, if you work all day, crating your dog is NOT an option.

You might say, "But he sleeps in there all night!" Yes, but night time is different. When a dog settles down to sleep at night, his metabolism (including his digestive system) slows down. Sleeping for 7 or 8 hours in his crate at night is fine.

But after he has slept all night, his metabolism returns to normal and he needs **activity**. You shouldn't head off to work and leave your dog in a crate. Even if you came home for lunch, that's not nearly enough.

A crate is simply too cramped for a dog to be stuck in for hours. In addition to the discomfort, he would be bored and terribly lonely.

Sociable animals like dogs shouldn't be kept isolated in a small space for hours, with only a brief visit and a quick walk at lunchtime.

If you work all day and already have your dog and he is either young (less than 2 years old) or has behavior issues such as barking or destructive chewing…

…well, you're faced with a difficult situation.

For that pup's own safety and to keep your house intact, he should be confined when you're gone. The solution—which is not a good one, but may be all that's possible—is to use a large wire *exercise pen* (Chapter 14) or else portable gates to confine your puppy to the kitchen or large laundry room.

If he absolutely must be alone for more than four hours a day, consider getting a second dog to keep him company. But not yet! Don't try to train two dogs *at the same time.* They will bond with each other and follow each other, rather than you.

Instead, work with the puppy you have, and once he is well-behaved, respectful, and housebroken, then look for another dog for companionship during those long lonely hours.

The second dog should not be a *puppy.* Puppies need tons of attention and training sprinkled throughout the day. They belong in homes where someone is home all day. Instead, I recommend adopting a good-natured adult dog of the opposite sex.

What size should the crate be?

 tall enough for your pup to sit and stand with a little clearance above his head.

 just wide enough for him to turn around in, and to lie down flat on his side.

 just deep enough so he can lie down on his stomach with his front paws stretched in front of him.

Now, if your puppy is a breed that will be much larger as an adult, there is a problem. Buying an adult-sized crate NOW means the puppy will likely sleep in one half of the crate and go to the bathroom in the other half. Not very desirable!

There are two solutions:

1. Buy an adult-sized crate that comes with a *divider*—a panel that lets you adjust the living space as your puppy grows. If you keep the living space small enough, you'll reduce the chances of the pup eliminating in one end and sleeping in the other.

2. Or buy a smaller crate now for housebreaking, and in a few months, after he's housebroken, buy a larger crate. Buying a smaller crate now means it's easier to move the crate around the house. This can be useful during the housebreaking period when the puppy spends so much time in the crate. It's nice to be able to move the crate to the room where you or the family is gathered.

What kind of crate is best?

For housebreaking, you want a plastic or wire crate. For already-housebroken pups, you might prefer a "luxury" (fashionable-looking) crate made of cloth, wood, or polymer. There are even indestructible aluminum crates for powerful chewers.

What I like about plastic crates:

 Plastic crates have a cozy, den-like atmosphere. They restrict your puppy's view of his surroundings, making him more likely to curl up and go to sleep.

 They're warmer inside, which can be nice if you keep your house temperature on the cool side and have a shivery breed.

What I don't like about plastic crates:

- They don't have a slide-out pan, so you must reach all the way inside the crate to clean it.

- You can't see your pup as well, so you can't tell exactly what he's doing in there.

- In hot weather, if you don't have air conditioning, plastic crates can be stuffy, which isn't good for short-faced breeds like Bulldogs and Pugs.

What I like about wire crates:

 The *Midwest LifeStages* crate comes with a divider to adjust the size of the living space. It has a slide-out pan for easier cleaning. You can clearly see what your pup is doing through the wire and there's air circulation in hot weather.

What I don't like about wire crates:

- Wire crates tend to clink and rattle. Their openness doesn't create that secure den atmosphere. When pups can see all around, they might be noisier and more energetic. (But you can buy a fitted crate cover, or drape a towel/ sheet over the top, back, and sides.)

Where should you put the crate?

- Don't place it where the sun can shine directly on it. It can get hot in there and cook your pup.

- Don't place it where air can blow on it from a heating/cooling register, a fan, or an air conditioner. Drafts are bad for dogs.

- Unless you're only going to use it as a nighttime sleeping spot, don't put it in an isolated area such as the utility room or laundry room.

Instead, try to put the crate where there is family activity going on. Typically that's the kitchen, living room, or family room. If you have an office/study where you spend much of the day, you might put the crate in there.

Or you can move it from room to room, though that will be a little more difficult if your pup is a Great Dane!

If you think a dog crate will be ugly in your home, don't despair. With a little thought, you can incorporate a crate into your decor by fitting it under an end table and/or camouflaging it with silk greenery. Just make sure the dog can't reach through the bars with his paws and pull anything chewable into the crate.

What should you put inside the crate?

Don't put a water bowl in the crate. It will spill, or the puppy will splash in it and make a mess. And drinking too much water just makes him need to pee more. Just make sure you offer plenty of drinks outside the crate throughout the day.

I put one toy in the crate during the day—usually a Nylabone® or hard rubber Kong® toy. But at night, no toys. You don't want your puppy practicing being active at night. You want him to sleep.

Adding bedding to the crate

If your pup is NOT housebroken:

Don't put anything soft in the crate. No towels, blankets, or soft beds. Why not? (1) Soft bedding can be chewed and swallowed, and intestinal blockages are life-threatening. (2) If a pup soils soft bedding, he's learning to eliminate on soft things, like your sofa or rug. (3) Soft bedding absorbs urine, which makes the puppy *more comfortable* when you actually want him to be a bit **uncomfortable,** as a subtle motivator to keep his crate clean.

For non-housebroken pups, I put newspapers in the crate. Yes, newspapers do absorb some urine and can be chewed, but pups are more likely to *shred* newspapers and less likely to eat them. Newspapers do make it easier to clean the crate.

> ☀️ **Don't put "housebreaking pads" (pee pads) in the crate.** These soft pads are sprayed with a chemical mixture that encourages pups to pee on them. You don't want to encourage your puppy to pee in his crate!

Once your pup is housebroken:

If he's not a chewer, add any comfortable bedding: thick towels or an imitation sheepskin bed. Remove labels and fringes to avoid nibbling. Moderate chewers often do okay with a "chew resistant" crate pad made of foam with a slick vinyl cover.

Serious chewer? I don't provide any soft bedding. Hopefully he will grow out of it with maturity, and then I'll try bedding.

How to put your puppy into the crate

Be sure he has had a potty break, followed by an activity session so he's ready for a rest. Of course, after the last potty break of the night, no activity session. He should be ready for bed by then.

Draw his attention to two or three tiny treats (cooked chicken works well) in your hand. Toss them into the middle of the crate and as he starts to go in after them, say cheerfully:

"Go crate" or "Go kennel."

He should go in at least far enough to eat the treats. Push the crate door against his bottom to move him the rest of the way in. Reach in and unsnap the leash. Close and latch the door. You want him to be calm, so use your low-key voice: "Good boy."

At bedtime, put him in his crate and go about your normal before-bed routine: turning off electronics, locking doors, pulling shades, etc. Don't talk to, or even look at, the puppy.

> You want him to learn the routine that once he is in his crate at bedtime, you won't be interacting with him any further. This is an important routine that encourages relaxation.

If your pup won't go into the crate

Some pups won't go into the crate even for treats. If possible (and safe), use the leash or your hands to guide him in, even if he's not thrilled about it.

If he's stronger than you or might bite, you'll need to move more slowly. At mealtime, add something aromatic to his food, such as steak or cheese. Put the bowl just inside the crate. Make sure the door is propped open so it can't close on him.

He might be stubborn enough to skip a meal or two, but he'll soon realize that he has to stick his head into the crate to eat, and hopefully he'll be tempted by the extra goodies.

Over a few days, slide the bowl farther back until finally he must enter the crate to eat. While he's eating, close the door for a minute or two before opening it again. (But if he vocalizes or tries to get out, wait until he stops before you let him out.)

If you work on this for a week, but you still can't get him into the crate, you might decide to give up and confine him in a small pen instead (Chapter 14).

> Just be aware that this degree of resistance isn't normal and points to something amiss in his psyche or in your leader-follower relationship, or both. It's likely that you will run into additional resistance as you continue training.

Teach your pup to "Wait" before he comes out of his crate.

The way you release your puppy from his crate is very important.

If you rush toward him, fling open the door, and welcome him out with hugs and exclamations of joy ("Yay! You're free!"), then the next time you put him in, he won't be able to relax. He will be **wired** the whole time, just itching to be released from "prison."

Instead, always let your puppy out in a calm, matter-of-fact way. As you walk toward the crate, don't speak to him. Open the door… but just a crack!

Hold out your hand like a stop sign and say, "Wait."

As you ease open the door, he might try to charge through the gap. Quickly close it so he can't come through. Don't slam(!) the door into him, but do close it fast enough to push him back.

Repeat your *hand signal* and "Wait" and ease open the door again. It doesn't need to reach the point where it's all the way open—just enough that he **could** fit through but he doesn't because he's responding to your "Wait". In the beginning, all you want is 3 to 5 seconds of restraint while the door is partially open.

You're teaching your puppy to control his impulses and wait for your permission. This is such a valuable lesson!

After those few successful seconds, reach in and snap on his leash. If he tries to rush out, block him with your hands or the door. Make sure he is waiting nicely before you say, "Okay", which is his cue to come out.

Depending on how large/old he is, you may want to scoop him up to carry him, or you may let him walk.

Carry him where? Let him walk where?

To his potty area. You want to establish the pattern that after being in the crate, he will always be able to go out to the bathroom. This pattern will help him "hold it" while he's in the crate.

So whether you're carrying him, or whether he's walking on his own, immediately head for the door to his potty area, saying, "You need to go **OUT?** Let's go **OUT.**"

If your puppy barks in his crate

Virtually all pups come to love the security of their crate. But in the beginning, when the crate is new and it's *your* idea that he should go in…and then you close the door…well, your pup may consider that whole experience to be a bummer.

So expect protesting at first. Barking, whining, whimpering. Make sure that no other pets (or kids) are inciting the puppy by running around near his crate or even just standing there staring at him.

Then pay no attention to the noise. *Don't talk to the puppy. Don't even look at him.* The noise should subside when he realizes that it's not working and that he might as well drift off to sleep or (during the day) chew on the toy you've given him.

However, some pups are more persistent and can make a fearsome racket. If you have close neighbors, obviously you can't let your pup howl for an hour. You need to step in before the neighbors (quite rightly) call your landlord, your homeowners association, or the police.

The first thing I do is to cover the crate with a sheet or towel so the puppy can't see out. When he can't see things happening, he's more likely to relax and settle down. Next, I put on soothing music: relaxing classical or mellow jazz.

If that doesn't help **and the pup is at least 10 weeks old, AS** he is in the middle of a bark/howl, say "No" or "AH-ah" and use one of the following corrective techniques:

 A harmless **spray of water** from a plastic spray bottle or squirt gun. Of course, the crate can't be covered for this one! You want him to learn this pattern: Vocalize → wet! So don't spray when he's being quiet.

If your pup doesn't seem to mind getting wet, try putting one hand on the crate and **giving it a wobble**, not enough to make him fall, just enough to unbalance him. This technique is often more effective when the crate is covered so the pup can't see your hand. You want him to think the wobble comes out of nowhere, caused entirely by his vocalizing.

 A sudden noise. In Chapter 5, I mentioned the Barker Breaker® by the *Amtek Company*, The Pet Corrector® by *The Company of Animals*, and The Pet Convincer® by *Canine Innovations*. These handheld devices produce a startling sound that can interrupt barking.

Under no circumstances—well, unless your house is on fire!— should you let a puppy out of his crate (or pen) when he is vocalizing, or immediately after he has been doing so.

> Make sure every family member understands that your pup must never be let out of the crate during (or immediately after) barking. Remember that dogs are very quick to recognize patterns! If he barks and you let him out, you are training him to bark whenever he wants out. Many, many owners make this mistake.

A general rule of thumb is that your pup should be quiet for at least 3 to 5 minutes before you let him out of the crate.

Children or other pets shouldn't be allowed to pester a puppy in his crate. As your dog's guardian, you must ensure that his time in his crate is peaceful and relaxing. Toddlers especially need to be monitored and taught that a pup is not to be disturbed in his crate.

Chapter 14

Stay Quietly in an Exercise Pen

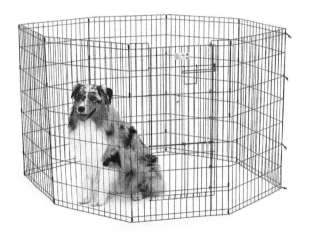

All pups should have a crate. Some pups should also have an exercise pen, especially pups who must stay alone for many hours, or who are being taught to use a litter box (Chapter 37).

An ex-pen is an indoor pen made of wire or plastic/vinyl. Typically you get eight panels hinged together to make a pen that's 4 feet wide by 4 feet long (16 square feet), which gives a puppy room to stretch his legs while still keeping him safely confined for a few hours. You can arrange the pen into a circle or a square.

You can get a pen 30-inches high (small breeds), 36-inches high, or 48-inches high. I like a brand called Midwest. You can search for *Midwest exercise pen* on Amazon.

If you don't like the look of wire, roverpet.com makes a nice-looking pen out of PVC white vinyl.

Most of my advice in the previous chapter on crates applies to ex-pens, as well: Where to place the pen, how to put your pup into the pen, how to take him out of the pen ("Wait" and "Okay"), and how to handle barking.

If your puppy jumps on the sides of the ex-pen

It's not uncommon for a dog to jump up on his hind legs and paw at the sides of the pen with his front paws. If he's young enough or small enough that the ex-pen stands firm, you can ignore this behavior at first. He's simply curious and exploring. Hopefully he will settle down and play with a toy.

But if he's larger and might knock over the pen with his jumping, you should correct it right away. Even if he's small, he shouldn't be repeatedly jumping. You want your pup to be calm and relaxed in his pen, not excitable.

Say "No" or "AH-ah" **AS** he jumps and use a corrective technique like the ones in the previous chapter for barking in the crate.

Chapter 15

"Wait" for Permission Before Going through Doors or Gates

Good news! You've already introduced this word. When you open your pup's crate or pen, instead of letting him charge out, you always have him *Wait* for a few seconds before releasing him with "Okay." Right?

Once a puppy is older than 10 weeks and behaves nicely on a leash (Chapter 11), I also show him how to *Wait* at doors and gates. He mustn't go through them without permission.

Why is this behavior so valuable? Well, let's see…

"Watch out for the dog!" Kathy cried. Her friend Mary Sue had just arrived and started to pull open the screen door so she could come into the kitchen.

Spotting the crack of daylight, Jake made a mad dash for it.

Mary Sue leaped backward and managed to slam the screen door a split-second before Jake barreled into it, leaving yet another nose print in the battered black mesh.

Mary Sue frowned through the screen at the exuberantly jumping dog. "What a nuisance!" she said to herself. "Why do they let him run through every open door?"

Why, indeed? Door-rushing behavior is unacceptable for several reasons:

- First, it could cost your pup his life. If he gets through the door and spies some temptation across the street—a cat or a squirrel—he might end up getting hit by a car.

- Second, it's unfair to your guests. Visitors shouldn't need to be paranoid about your puppy barreling past them. As our dogs' guardians, it's our responsibility to teach them to stay put, even when a door or gate tempts them.

- Third, it's a calmness issue. Your pup needs to learn to control his impulses even when distractions tempt him.

- Finally, it's a leadership issue. *Wait* requires your puppy to acknowledge your existence, to look to you for direction, to wait for **your** permission before doing something he wants to do.

Some trainers teach this behavior without using the word "Wait." In other words, they teach the pup to wait automatically at every door and gate, to never go through unless they hear "Okay."

You can choose to teach it either way: with or without a command. I start with the word and phase it out later when it's obvious the pup no longer needs it.

How to teach "Wait" at the door

1. You're indoors, with your pup on leash. Walk toward the front door. (If there's also a screen door, prop the screen open ahead of time so it won't be blocking you when you open the front door.)

2. Put your hand on the doorknob and say, "Wait." Pronounce the word *crisply.*

Pronounce that "t" at the end—wai**T**. Don't ask "Wait?" as though you're asking him a question.

3. Open the door. If your puppy tries to rush out, use the *Loosen-Tug* technique you learned in Chapter 11 to bring him back inside.

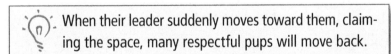 Be quick! Don't let him get all the way through the door before you pull him back. As soon as one front foot goes over the threshold, pull him back, and as soon as his foot comes back inside, loosen the leash so that the clip is hanging straight down.

Now it's all about repetition. Keep giving him the opportunity to move over the threshold by loosening the leash. If he makes that choice, repeat your leash technique.

You can also use **spatial pressure** to discourage a pup from crossing the threshold. That means crowding him with your body, even bumping him slightly with your leg to make him move back and away from the threshold. Trainers call this "claiming space."

When their leader suddenly moves toward them, claiming the space, many respectful pups will move back.

When he stops trying to cross the threshold and stands there on a loose leash...

 Say, "Yes. Good boy." Give him a treat. Close the door. Repeat. When you can open the door without him trying to go through at all, say, "Okay" and go out for your walk.

> From now on, whenever you take your pup for a walk, have him "Wait" inside the open door for 5–10 seconds until you say, "Okay."

"Wait" with distractions

Once a pup is *Waiting* nicely and is more than 6 months old, I like to add distractions. Assume the front door is open and your pup is standing there with you on a loose leash.

✓ Hum or whistle. Do a few knee bends or jumping jacks. Sit in a chair near the door (inside the house) and read aloud from a book. Talk to an imaginary visitor at the door.

What should your puppy be doing during this time? Well, he can stand near the open door, or he can sit or lie down, or walk around within the limits of the leash. His choice. He just can't put his foot over the threshold. No barking or pulling on the leash, either.

Is he still waiting? Great! Don't forget to praise, calmly. Don't get him all excited.

Wait on a long leash

After days of practice, swap his 6-foot leash for a long (15- to 20-foot) leash or cord. Now with your front door wide open, you can wander around the room holding the cord. Your pup can follow you around if he wants, or he can hang out near the open door, looking and sniffing. He just can't cross the threshold.

Wait while YOU go outside

After more days of practice, go back to his regular leash. With the front door open and both of you standing inside the house, repeat "Wait" and then **YOU** step over the threshold.

You want him to stay on his side, so help him at first by keeping gentle tension on the leash—upward and backward—as you step through, to help hold your pup on HIS side of the door. This is new to him and you want him to succeed!

As soon as your foot hits the ground outside, turn and face him. Now he should be inside the house and you should be just outside, on the porch or stoop, holding tension on the leash to keep him indoors.

Caution him again to "Wait" and loosen the leash. I hold up my hand like a stop sign. If he tries to join you outside, the moment his foot crosses the threshold, use the leash to guide/slide him back inside the house.

You stay put on your side. Once he's back inside, caution him again and loosen the leash, giving him another chance to either rush out or stay put.

No matter how many times you have to guide him back inside, when he does finally stand there—actually, he can stand or sit or lie down or even walk back and forth, just so long as he stays on his side of the threshold—he has just done a marvelous *Wait*. Praise him calmly (but don't let him cross the threshold yet).

Finally, say, "Okay" and let him come across.

But not always! Instead of always letting him come outside to join you, sometimes you should go back inside the house and close the door.

In other words, **don't always** give him an "Okay" to come out. In practical life, you will sometimes need to go outside for a moment by yourself—say, to sign for a package. Then you'll go back inside without your pup ever being allowed out. So he should learn early on that he doesn't always get to cross the boundary after "Wait."

 Teaching your puppy to look to you for direction and guidance is immensely reassuring to him!

Other places to practice "Wait"

 Have your pup "Wait" before going INTO your house. For example, when you return to your house after a walk, say "Wait" and open the front door but don't let him go IN until you've given the "Okay."

 Have him "Wait" at the back door before you let him out into the yard.

 Have him "Wait" before going through the sliding doors to the patio.

 Have him "Wait" before going in—or out—of the gate to your property.

 Don't ask your puppy to "Wait" OFF LEASH anywhere where he could dash into the street. A pup will always choose the worst possible moment to forget or ignore a word—and all it takes is once for your pup to be dead.

Chapter 16

"Go to Your Bed"

"Place" or "Go place" or "Go to your bed" is one of the most powerful commands to teach your puppy. His *Place* is a designated dog bed or blanket to which he should go when told.

When you want him to go there, you gesture toward the bed and say, "Jake, **go place**" (or one of the other phrases above).

For this exercise, your pup should be at least 10 or 12 weeks old and should behave nicely on a leash.

You might wonder if *Place* could refer to his crate. It could. But when I want my dog to go into his crate, I say "Go crate."

I use, "Go place" or "Go to your bed" to refer to an open dog bed placed somewhere in the room.

You can even move his *Place* from room to room. For example, if you're watching TV, put his bed there so he can hang out with you.

When you head for your den to work on your computer, carry his bed to the den.

Or you can have different beds in different rooms.

Three reasons why "Place" is one of the most powerful commands to teach your puppy

1. *Place* **is calming.** When your pup must hang out on his bed and not walk away from it, he learns patience and impulse control, two qualities that are essential for young, energetic, or excitable pups to learn. *Place* becomes almost a meditative experience. The pup learns to relax his body and calm his mind even when the world keeps churning around him. He learns to ignore kids playing, the phone ringing, the vacuum cleaner, the mailman.

> Many dogs with behavior issues are completely turned around by learning *Place.* Dogs with phobias, anxieties, and noise sensitivities dramatically improve when they're required to control themselves on their bed. It doesn't happen immediately. But in a comparatively short time, you'll see the difference.

2. *Place* **is practical.** Instead of letting a young or mischievous dog loose in the house, free to practice bad habits, you can let him hang out with you in a safe space—his bed. Sure, you could put him in his crate or pen, but if he knows how to relax on his comfortable bed, he can stay right out in the open with you, wherever you are.

3. *Place* **shows your pup that you're in control.** He learns that sometimes he needs to do something simply because you say

so. He must stay there quietly, just watching the world go by, *because you want him to.*

Place is one of the easiest commands to teach.

For most pups, the best kind of bed for teaching *Place* is an elevated bed. Either a hammock-style bed, like this one by K&H Products...

 ...or a raised bed like this Petfusion® memory foam. I like an elevated bed because it's so obvious when the dog is ON it, and when he's not.

Or you can use a flat bed with rounded bolsters around the edge to help define the bed. Very small pups often prefer it because it's right on the ground, so they don't need to hop up onto it.

To start teaching *Place,* position the bed in the middle of a room (rather than in a corner or against a wall) so you and your pup can easily walk around it. Or practice in your yard.

Of course he should be on leash. As you approach the bed together, say, "Place" or whichever word or phrase you're going to use. Everyone in your household should say the same thing.

Gesture toward the bed and use the leash to gently steer your puppy onto the bed. The moment all four feet are on the bed, say, "Yes!" or "Good!" and give him a treat *while he's on the bed.* Then say "Okay" and walk away with him. Repeat many times.

Your pup won't get on the bed?

If gentle guidance with the leash doesn't work, break the exercise into easy-to-master bits. Spend some time just walking him over to the bed and dropping a treat on it. If he reaches onto the bed to eat it, say "Yes!" or "Good!" and hand him another treat. Then walk away, turn around, and come back for another pass.

Eventually maneuver him so that the bed is between the two of you and put a little pressure on the leash to encourage him to walk across the bed to your side. If he puts even *one foot* onto the bed, say "Yes!" or "Good!" and treat. After several successes with one foot, withhold your praise/treat until he puts **both front feet** on the bed, and so on.

What should your puppy DO when he's on the bed?

At first, nothing. Simply walk him on, praise/treat, say "Okay," and walk him off.

When you think he's ready to stay longer, say "Yes or "Good" when he gets on the bed and give him the treat. But instead of saying "Okay" and walking away with him, just stand there.

If he tries to step off the bed, use the leash to gently stop him. Then loosen it again. Check him gently with the leash, then loosen it, as many times as necessary until he shows understanding that he's supposed to stay there.

When you're first teaching this exercise, you should only ask your dog to stay on the bed for a few seconds. Then say, "Okay" and walk him off. He must wait for your "Okay" before stepping off.

Now it's just a matter of gradually increasing the time he needs to stay on the bed before you give him the release word.

> :bulb: **Important:** Your puppy doesn't need to lie down on the bed. He can if he wants to, but he can also sit or stand or move around. He simply can't get off the bed. No barking either.

Circle around the bed while your puppy stays on it.

Some pups try to step off the bed when you move. So the first few times you try it, raise the leash vertically above your pup's head with a bit of gentle tension to remind him to stay on.

I like to place my left hand, palm **UP,** above the dog's head, then drape the leash across my palm between my thumb and index finger. Then I can just quickly raise my palm to check him with the leash if he tries to step off.

Stay close beside the bed as you circle it. It's fine if your pup moves around *on* the bed as you move *around* the bed. But he should not step off until you say "Okay."

> Patience and persistence are the keys to this very important exercise. If *YOU* don't give up, your puppy will eventually sigh and stay on the bed, and as far as leadership goes, you will have just taken a giant step forward in his eyes.

Add distractions.

Once your puppy will *reliably* stay on the bed for up to a minute, add the same kinds of distractions you used for teaching *Wait:*

✓ Hum or whistle. Do a few knee bends or jumping jacks. Read aloud from a book. Walk in circles around the bed.

Don't TEASE the dog. For example, don't pat your thighs to encourage him to come to you. Don't speak to him or even look at him. You're not trying to make him fail. You're trying to build up his confidence that he CAN stay on the bed.

As he gets more reliable, you can progress to sitting in a chair and reading a book. But keep an eye on him. You don't want him wandering around the room while you're engrossed in your book!

Eventually (though not when your pup is only a few months old!), you'll be able to leave the room and return to find him still on his *Place*. What a marvelous exercise in self-control!

How long can your puppy stay on his Place?

I don't start teaching *Place* until a pup is 10 or 12 weeks old, and then I only have him stay on his bed for a minute or two. I push that up to 15–30 minutes for pups 3 to 6 months old. Pups over 6 months can stay on their bed for an hour.

If you're laughing out loud at the idea that your 8-month-old pup could hang around on his bed for an hour...**then he is the perfect candidate for learning how.**

Because any pup who feels secure and stress-free is perfectly able to relax for an hour or two on a comfy bed in a comfy house with his trusted leader close by. If your dog can't, that's strong evidence that he is feeling too anxious, too "wired," to be truly secure and stress-free.

> When you teach him how to relax and be calm, his stress levels will go way down and his contentment levels will go way up. *Place* is the perfect lesson to make that happen.

In fact, it's often *easier* for a dog to stay on his bed for an hour than to stay for just a few minutes.

You see, if he learns that he only needs to wait 20 seconds and then you'll let him up, he'll be tensed up the whole time. He'll stare at you, shift restlessly, and tighten his muscles whenever you look in his direction. He's waiting for the slightest sign that he can explode off his bed and be free, free, free!

Not very calming or meditative, is it?

However, over an hour, most pups relax and go to sleep.

But let's say your pup doesn't go to sleep, at least not right away.

What if he stares at you?

Don't make eye contact. Most puppies interpret eye contact as an invitation to interact with you. In fact, your pup may try hard to make eye contact so he can assume his most charming or pathetic expression and persuade you to stop this nonsense and play with him instead.

What if he inches farther and farther off the bed?

He might start by hanging his front paws off the edge. "There, that didn't hurt anything, did it? After all, most of me is still on the bed!"

Then he's stretching one paw until it touches the floor. "Ooh, it feels good to stretch. How about another inch? How about two inches…"

You can see where this is headed, right? This is why I prefer elevated beds for teaching *Place,* because it's easier to see when the dog has come so far off the bed that he's touching the floor. With other beds, it's more of a judgment call as to when he is **on** versus **off.**

In any case, when he seems **off** to you, use the leash to scoot him back on. Also be sure not to give him any treats if you have to put him back on the bed. You don't want him to learn this pattern: leave bed → get put back on bed → get a treat! Puppies will quickly learn the worst patterns!

What if he tries to chew on the bed (or the leash)? What if he whines or barks?

"No. AH-ah." Follow up with a corrective technique. You know the common ones by now, so pick whatever works for your pup.

What if he rolls on his back with all four feet in the air?

Ha-ha! That's fine. All he has to do is stay on the bed, quietly and peacefully. That looks pretty quiet and peaceful to me!

Releasing your pup from his Place

Only use *Place* **when you're sure you will remember** to keep a close eye on your puppy. If you get called away for anything important, first release your pup with "Okay" and get him off the bed before you go answer it.

Otherwise, when he's first learning this exercise, he'll probably walk off the bed while you're busy elsewhere. That's not good for your leader-follower relationship. Once you've put him on his *Place*, he needs to wait for YOU to release him.

Using Place to "soundproof" your puppy

Once a puppy shows that he fully understands his responsibility to stay on the bed for an extended period of time, I add *sound effects.*

Every pup should be able to relax even when he hears fireworks, thunderstorms, other dogs barking, a baby crying, kids squealing and playing, a vacuum cleaner, construction equipment, traffic sounds, and emergency vehicle sirens.

Sadly, many pups are hypersensitive and hyperreactive to harmless sounds. Some breeds tend to be more sound sensitive than others, so clearly there is a genetic component.

But more commonly, sound sensitivity is caused by owners who respond improperly when the pup acts worried or nervous. Typically, owners respond by trying to reassure the puppy with soothing words and petting.

Unfortunately, that's the worst thing to do. A soothing voice and petting are interpreted by dogs as **positive reinforcement** of whatever behavior they're exhibiting at the time. If you reward nervous behavior, you're going to see **more** nervous behavior.

 Owners who soothe and pet and cuddle a worried dog aren't helping the dog, but actually making things worse.

I recommend using *Place* to prevent sound sensitivity from developing in your dog. Or if you already have a pup with this problem, you can use *Place* to help the pup overcome it.

Get hold of a sound effects CD such as *Calm Pet: Desensitizing Sounds* or *Sounds for Hounds*. Or find free sound effects on YouTube. Try to include all the sounds I mentioned earlier.

Play these sounds for 10–15 minutes a day while your puppy is on his *Place*. The first week the volume should be so low as to be barely audible. **If the pup ignores the sounds,** walk over a couple of times and give him a treat. This helps him associate **hearing and ignoring sounds** with **rewards**.

The following week, increase the volume a bit, and so on.

If he acts fearful (cowering or shaking) but stays on the bed, reduce the volume for a few days. Other than that, *ignore* the fearfulness. Don't speak to him, look at him, or give any treats.

Whether fearful or not, **if he gets off his bed,** say, "No" or "AH-ah", give the leash a mild corrective tug, and lead him back on.

If he keeps getting off and running into another room, move the bed near a heavy piece of furniture to which you can attach the leash. Make it very short so he can't get far off the bed. Of course you will be right there in the room with him and can quickly usher him back onto his bed.

What you're doing is removing his opportunities to practice poor coping skills such as running away, hiding, pacing, or coming to you for cuddling. Allowing him to choose any of those options only makes the situation grow progressively worse.

When you remove those options by requiring him to stay on the bed, he might still cower and shake for quite some time. But as the sounds become more familiar, and as he focuses more on his responsibility to stay on the bed, he will work through his fear and develop much better coping skills.

Yes, you're stressing the pup. But imagine the stress he would experience throughout his life whenever something frightened him and he had no coping skills other than running away. We don't help our dogs by avoiding all stress in their lives. We help them by exposing them to stress in a safe, controlled environment and teaching them to cope calmly with it. Dogs with "issues" can't grow or change unless they're nudged out of their comfort zone. Working through something they didn't think they could do builds confidence and is satisfying and empowering to dogs. To us, too.

Chapter 17

Your Puppy Should Look at You When You Say His Name

The most obvious word you want your puppy to learn is his name. You want him to recognize that a particular sound means **HIM.** You want him to look at you when he hears that sound.

Haven't named your puppy yet?

Here's my advice:

 It's easier for a dog to learn a one- or two-syllable name (Luke, Jenna, Kelly). If you're partial to a longer name, try to choose one that can be shortened. For example, his full name might be Cappuccino but you call him Cap or Cappy.

 Avoid names that rhyme with No (Beau, Joe, Coco) or that start with No (Nova, Noel, Noble).

 Avoid unflattering names like Dumbo, Trouble, Devil, Killer. Of course the dog doesn't understand the meaning, but *people* do, and every time you or anyone else says that name, it's only natural to think of him as being dumb or troublemaking or aggressive. That can come across in your body language and your dog may give you exactly what you expect. So try to pick a positive name.

Step #1 of teaching your puppy his name

Put a handful of soft treats in your pocket. Most pups love cooked chicken: tiny pieces, less than half the size of your thumbnail.

Find a quiet room indoors without distractions. If you have small children or other pets, put them in another room.

Stand in the quiet spot with your puppy on leash. Because you're just standing there saying and doing nothing, he will probably get bored and look up at you. Immediately call his name in a happy voice: "Jake!" (don't just *say* it—*call* it) and give him a treat.

Wait for his attention to wander. Walk around the room if that gets him to look away from you. Then stop and wait for him to look up at you again. When he does so, call "Jake!" and give him a treat.

Repeat this pattern about 10 times.

> But there's a problem, isn't there? Your pup isn't looking away from you anymore!

Remember, dogs are *opportunists* who repeat behaviors that bring them something good. Your pup won't take his eyes off you right now because he has made the connection that **looking at you** produces a treat. So of course he doesn't want to look away.

That's perfectly okay. If he won't look away, just call his name **while** he's looking at you. Then give the treat. You're still teaching him that his name is associated with something really good.

Also, there should be times during the day when you're walking or playing with your puppy and he happens to look attentively at you or walk toward you.

That's a good time to connect those behaviors with his name by calling, "Jake!" and praising him ("Good boy!").

Step #2 of teaching your puppy his name

Don't be in a rush to move on to this step. Many owners make the mistake of standing across the kitchen and calling their puppy's name while he's busy doing something else. He might hear the *jake* sound, but he's too distracted to respond to it. Then the owner just stands there and does nothing. Which only reinforces in the pup's mind that the *jake* sound must be meaningless.

So give him lots and lots of opportunities to hear the *jake* sound when he's actually looking at you, so he learns the pattern that the sound refers to **himself.**

When you're ready to try calling his name when he's looking away from you, have him on leash. Walk around the inside of your house or yard with your pup. When he gets distracted and looks toward something that interests him, call his name.

If he doesn't immediately look in your direction, call his name again and take a few steps backward, tightening the leash. This should make him look toward you. Then you can praise ("Good boy! Yay!") and treat.

It shouldn't be long before your puppy looks at you immediately when you say his name. Then start cutting back on the treats. Reward for the first look, and the second look. For the third look, praise but give no treat. So it's treat, treat, no treat. Then cut back to treat, no treat, treat, no treat.

Finally, make the treats random. You might treat twice in a row, then nothing three times in a row, then treat, then nothing. Mix it up so your pup's good behavior isn't dependent on treats.

Do's and don'ts when teaching your puppy his name

 Watch for opportunities during the day to use your pup's name *whenever he heads toward you.*

 Don't call his name when you're going to correct him.

 Don't use his name in combination with *No.* "Jake, good boy!" is fine. "Jake, no!" is less good.

Unfortunately, though, when you have multiple dogs milling around, sometimes you do need to use the name of the misbehaving one so the other dogs don't feel corrected when they haven't done anything wrong.

Chapter 18

Come When Called

Along with "Good" and "No," which tell your puppy which behaviors you want and which behaviors you don't want, the most important word in his vocabulary is "Come."

Unlike fun tricks such as "Shake hands" or "Play dead," where it doesn't really matter whether your puppy learns it or not…

"Come" is a mandatory word that must be mastered.

> For the rest of your dog's life, he should never hear the word "Come" without being required to obey it. Dogs who fail to come when called have been *allowed* to learn that pattern. In the beginning, you need a leash to guarantee that your dog comes every single time he hears the word.

Step #1 in teaching "Come"

1. Put a handful of treats in your pocket, and with your puppy on leash, wander around your house or yard. When his attention is elsewhere (for example, when he is sniffing something), stop walking and say his name: "Jake!"

This sounds familiar, doesn't it? You did this when you were teaching your pup his name (Chapter 17).

2. When he turns to look at you in response to his name, call in a happy voice, "Come!" Trot backward a few steps, crouch down, and pat your hands together or pat your hands on your thighs.

3. The instant he starts toward you, praise and encourage him, "Yes! Come!" Make sure the leash hangs completely loose as he comes toward you—don't reel him in like a fish!

4. As he approaches you, don't reach out to grab him. Keep encouraging him with your hands and voice to come all the way to you. Praise, pet, and treat. Then "Okay!" which means he doesn't need to stay near you any longer.

But what if...?

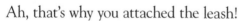

- What if he doesn't come toward you when you say "Come"?

- Or what if he comes partway, but stops?

- Or what if he comes toward you, but runs past?

Ah, that's why you attached the leash!

Use the leash to guide him to you, praising the whole way: "Yes! Come!" When he arrives, praise, pet, and treat.

 You want him to **always succeed** at doing the action that fits the word.

 And you want him to learn that **coming close to you** is always associated with goodness!

> Practice indoors. Practice outdoors in your yard. Keep the leash on so he MUST come. Give him dozens of experiences hearing the word "Come!" and coming toward you.

Step #2 in teaching "Come"

Switch to a long (15- to 30-foot) line. Wander around the yard with him, calling him when he's at the end of the line. After a while, drop your end of the line and let him drag it around. If you call him and he doesn't come, you can easily step on the line.

When he's so reliable that you would place a bet on him coming whenever you call, switch back to his regular leash and drop your end. Now if he doesn't come, you'll have a harder time getting hold of that short leash. So don't do this step too soon!

Suppose you DO drop the leash too soon and you call him and he doesn't come. Try one more call, in a firmer tone of voice.

If he still doesn't come, don't say another word. GO GET HIM.

As you walk toward your disobedient pup, he may move away from you, even run away from you.

Don't run after him. Don't say anything. Just track him down silently. Walk firmly and purposefully. Keep your eyes fixed on him. Baffled and unnerved by your persistent, methodical following, your pup will most likely shrink down and give up. Or you will get close enough to step on the end of the leash.

So whether he just stands there waiting for you or you have to track him down, the goal is to get hold of his leash.

Once you have the leash in your hand, give it a good *pop* to propel him in your direction. Then start trotting backward, saying, "Come! Come!" Your voice should be quite firm here, not cheerful. After all this time, he knows what *Come* means. He chose to ignore it and you need to hold him accountable for his choices.

After backing up a bit and using the leash to make sure he is coming toward you the whole time, it's time to stop and **change your attitude dramatically.** Smile! Praise him! Pet him! Scoop him up, if he's small! Do whatever it takes to get his tail wagging!

The message you want to send is this:

> *"Whenever you come to me,* I am the ultimate happy place, full of praise and petting and perhaps a treat. *Come to me* and it's always good. If you don't come to me, I will track you down to the ends of the earth and I'll **make** you come to me. Now, wouldn't you rather do it the easy way?"

This is a critical lesson for your pup to learn. One way or the other he has to do what you say, and doing it immediately, on his own, is much more comfortable and pleasant than being made to do it.

Chapter 19

Take Things Gently from Your Hand

When food appears, many dogs are so eager to grab it that they become oblivious to your existence.

With this simple routine, you teach your pup that treats do not fall from the sky to be snatched up the instant he sees one.

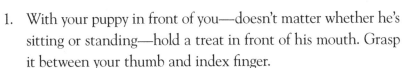

Rather, treats come *from the leader's hand*, which should be "treated" (pun intended!) with respect.

1. With your puppy in front of you—doesn't matter whether he's sitting or standing—hold a treat in front of his mouth. Grasp it between your thumb and index finger.

> Don't hold it too high, else he'll jump for it, which is not the calm behavior you're trying to teach.

2. Say, "EEEE-zee." Draw it out as a long cautionary word. If he tries to snatch at it, say, "AH-Ah" and either (a) pull it back or

(b) leave your hand where it is but twist/rotate it so he only sees the back of your hand and can't see or reach the treat. Caution again, "EEEE-zee" and give him another chance to be polite.

3. You should see his facial expression change when he realizes that you won't let him grab with his whole mouth. He should then reach out carefully and take the treat gently, using his front teeth.

4. Only release the treat when he takes it gently. Add a single soothing "Goooood" as he takes it nicely.

> This **gentleness routine** helps your puppy pay closer attention to your existence and treat you with thoughtful respect.

"Easy" is a word you'll use in other circumstances, too. It's a **control word** that cautions your pup to be calm and gentle. You can use it when you introduce him to something that he must be careful with (like a new kitten) so that he doesn't get excitable or engage in rough play.

Chapter 20

Take Charge of Your Pup's Food

One of the best ways to establish a good leader-follower relationship with your puppy is by controlling *resources.* Resources are things your pup views as important, such as food, toys, sleeping spots, even petting and belly rubs.

Most dogs view FOOD as the most important resource. When you show your pup that you're in charge of the food, you're making the gentle but clear statement that you are the leader and he is the follower. Your puppy finds this very reassuring.

How do you show him that you're in charge of the food? As with most leadership techniques, it's simply a matter of making the right routine that your pup can count on.

First, how often should you feed your pup?

Most puppies over 8 weeks old should eat three meals per day until 4 months old, then two meals per day thereafter.

Toy breed puppies (because they can have problems regulating their blood sugar) should eat four meals per day until 4 months old, then three meals per day until 6 months old, then two meals per day thereafter.

Adult dogs should eat twice a day unless they have health problems that require more meals.

Dogs who eat only once a day may experience an empty stomach, may even spit up white froth or bile. Think of how our own stomachs growl and how we feel irritable when we've gone many hours without eating.

WHAT to feed your puppy is a more complicated question that I address in my canine health book, *11 Things You Must Do Right To Keep Your Dog Healthy and Happy.*

A good mealtime routine

 Cue your pup when you're ready to prepare his meal. "Are you **hungry?** Want your **food?**" Exaggerate the key words.

 Have him come with you to the kitchen. Get his bowl from the same cupboard and set it on the same counter every time. He should be right there watching you. You want him to see that **YOU** are the source of his food.

 If he's acting excitable, don't put his food down, else he'll learn that excitable behavior makes the food appear! If he's racing around, barking, or jumping, he should be on leash so you can control him. Barking corrections are in Chapter 24. Jumping corrections are in Chapter 25.

 When he is calm, the bowl is ready to go down. If he already knows how to sit (Chapter 31), have him sit first—another subtle and gentle leadership thing. Then…"Okay!" and place the bowl on the floor, in the same spot every time. "Here's your **food.**"

If you have multiple dogs, each should have his own eating spot away from the others. Place the bowls down in the same order each time, saying the dog's name as his bowl goes down. "Buffy…here's your *food*. Kelly…*food.*"

 During mealtime, leaders protect followers. Don't let kids or other pets approach a dog who is eating. If one of your dogs is not well-behaved enough to obey this rule, he should be dragging his leash so you can get hold of him. If necessary, feed the dogs in separate crates or separate rooms. Stealing food is completely unacceptable.

 If a pup walks away from his bowl, pick it up. If there is still food left, make a mental or written note, as it could suggest illness.

After 10 minutes, all the bowls should be picked up to avoid picky behavior or food guarding.

The final part of the routine is a potty break immediately after every meal. If you're still housebreaking, take the pup out on leash. If he's already **100%** housebroken and eliminates reliably when you send him out himself, that's fine.

In either case, announce the potty break: "Do you need to go **OUT?** Time to go **OUT.**"

No scheduled mealtimes? You leave kibble down all day?

Oops, that's not a good idea. You shouldn't even leave food down for an hour, let alone all day.

> Remember: the easiest way to raise and train your puppy is to establish choreographed routines—same things, same order, same words—with yourself as the director, the one in charge. Create good routines, stick to them, and your pup's behavior will be predictable and good.

Here are 5 reasons "free feeding" is not a good idea:

1. Free feeding can create picky eaters who feel **entitled** to food rather than appreciative of being given food.

2. Free feeding makes your pup's digestive cycle **unpredictable,** which means you don't know when he will need to go to the bathroom.

3. Your pup's **appetite** is a good barometer of his **health,** and it's easier to keep tabs on appetite when you're offering scheduled meals and watching him eat.

4. If you have more than one dog, free feeding invites bullying and can create food-guarding issues.

5. Finally, as you've seen in this chapter, **scheduled** feeding is a prime opportunity to demonstrate that you are in charge of the food. You make the food appear, you require your pup to be calm and polite before you give it to him, you allow a certain amount of time for eating, then you pick up the bowl.

> Scheduled, controlled feeding reinforces the subtle leader-follower relationship, whereas "free feeding" gives your puppy the impression that food is always magically available.

Should you pick up your pup's food bowl while he's eating, to teach him that you can take his food away?

On this issue, my fellow trainers are divided.

Some say, "Yes, you should teach your pup that you can take his food away. Someday you might need to do that to keep him safe."

Others say, "Taking your pup's bowl away can *cause* anxiety and food guarding. Let him eat in peace."

I see the merits of both views, and I do something in-between.

When I have a new puppy, I *do* accustom him to having my hand near his bowl. I do this by walking past him while he's eating and casually dropping something extra-yummy (chicken or cheese) into his bowl. I say, "Good *food*" as I do so.

I do this once or twice a week, then at some point while he's eating, I say, "Want some *food?*" and I pick up the bowl he's eating from. I only raise it a foot or two off the floor and I make sure that he sees me add a yummy treat. "Good *food*," I say as I give the bowl back.

> I do this only once every couple of months, no more. This positive technique turns the removal of his food bowl into a good thing. Then if you should need to take it completely away, it's more likely that he won't react negatively. (More likely, but not guaranteed!)

If your dog is already guarding his food

If you approach your pup while he's eating and he...

- stops eating and stares fixedly at you

- pushes his head deep into the bowl and freezes his body

- braces his front legs on either side of the bowl as though claiming it

- or curls his lip or growls

...you have a problem. It's called *resource guarding* **and it's a potentially dangerous behavior issue.**

What should you do? Well, judgment is required here.

If your pup is large or if he has already snapped at someone, you should call a local **balanced** trainer who can evaluate the situation personally. If the pup is smallish and has never snapped at anyone, you might decide to try working with him on your own. The good news is that some resource guarding will stop simply by establishing the right leader-follower relationship.

Work through everything on the *Cheat Sheet* in Chapter 4. The pup should not be allowed on your bed or furniture (Chapter 21). He should not be allowed to demand petting (Chapter 22). He should *Wait* for your permission before going through any door or gate (Chapter 15). Give only one toy (Chapter 29), but take even that away if he makes any attempt to guard it.

In addition, feed the pup in his crate. Put the food in first, then move well away from the crate and send the pup in. When he's done, call the pup out and make sure he's well away from the crate before you remove the bowl.

Always think *safety.*

Alternatively, you can completely change the way you feed the pup. Put away his bowl. Feed him by offering one small scoop at a time from a long-handled spoon. Before each bite, have him Sit or Down or Come or any other word that he knows. **In other words, he must work for his food.**

If you do all that but see no improvement, I strongly urge you to find a local balanced trainer who can (safely) teach the pup to move away from the bowl when told to.

> This is a serious issue. Many dogs get dropped off at shelters or offered *free to good home* because they're resource guarders. Many biting dogs started out as resource guarders of food or toys (Chapter 29) or sleeping spots (Chapter 21). Some dogs even view their owner's lap as a resource to be guarded (Chapter 22).

I hope it goes without saying that you should not allow a child around a pup who is a resource guarder.

Chapter 21

Take Charge of Where Your Pup Rests and Sleeps

When an owner calls me about a behavior problem with her puppy, one of my first questions is, "Where does he sleep?"

The most common answer is, "In our bed" or "In bed with one of the kids."

My next question is, "Does he get up on the furniture?" Again the usual answer is yes.

Now, don't get me wrong! The majority of dogs who sleep on their owner's bed or furniture are perfectly well-behaved.

But when we look at dogs who HAVE behavior issues, most of those dogs also sleep on the bed or furniture.

Why is that important? Because we begin solving behavior issues by establishing the proper leader-follower relationship with your pup. And one of the best ways to establish that relationship is to control resources.

In the last chapter, you learned that *from a canine perspective,* the leader of a family or group controls the resources. *Food* is a resource. **So are *sleeping spots.*** The leader gets the choice sleeping spots. The followers sleep in spots that are less good. The way your dog views the world, that's a perfectly normal arrangement.

So if a puppy has behavior problems, one of the best ways to earn his respect is for you to reserve the best sleeping spots for yourself. You (and the other humans in your family) sleep on the beds and sit on the furniture.

Your *follower* pup rests and sleeps in his crate, or on a dog bed, or on the floor.

> It might seem like a simple thing to us, but when you control the sleeping spots, a canine finds that quite impressive! It's so easy to earn your pup's respect by taking small, simple actions that say, "I am the leader and you are the follower."

Is it ever okay for a dog to sleep on your bed?

Sure! If your dog is...

 an adult,

 100% housebroken,

 respectful of you and your spouse, and

 has no behavior issues.

What about sleeping with the kids?

That should require even **better** behavior. The dog should meet all the criteria above AND be polite with the kids—no jumping on them, nipping, or grabbing food or toys from their hands.

Even if your dog meets all the criteria above, there are other reasons you might not want him sleeping in your bed:

1. A small dog could get hurt by jumping or rolling off the bed in the dark.

2. A dog who sleeps on your bed could come to view you more like a littermate than a leader. That's the last thing you need if you're trying to *enhance* your leadership image. Some owners make things worse by trying not to "disturb" the sleeping pup. If you roll over and the pup groans or opens one eye and you stop moving, this unfortunate pattern might progress to a grumble or growl if you bump into him.

3. If you're married, a dog on your bed may position himself, deliberately or accidentally, between you and your spouse. Um… psychologically, that's not good.

> So it's up to you. Personally, I prefer my dogs to be safe and secure in their crates or pens at night. But I've also had dogs sleeping on my bed—always fully housebroken, respectful adult dogs with no behavior issues.

Should you let your dog on your furniture?

Again, a dog who is an adult, housebroken, respectful, and has no behavior problems…sure. My dogs are allowed on the furniture. But they didn't *start out* allowed on the furniture!

- A dog who is not housebroken? **NO.** Non-housebroken dogs are easily tempted to pee on soft cushy surfaces.

- A dog with respect issues or behavior problems? **NO.** Not until those issues clear up. Many of these pups have come to view sleeping on the furniture as a **right** rather than a privilege.

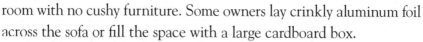

Restricting the furniture to humans elevates those humans in the eyes of the dog. That is a psychologically healthy attitude for a pup to have, especially when he has behavior issues.

If your puppy tries to sneak onto the furniture, keep a leash on him in the house so you can shoo him off. When you're gone, put him in a crate or pen, or in a gated room with no cushy furniture. Some owners lay crinkly aluminum foil across the sofa or fill the space with a large cardboard box.

Or try a *PetSafe ScatMat,* which is a flexible vinyl mat that you spread on the sofa. If your pup jumps on it, he feels a low-voltage static pulse (like we feel when we touch a doorknob after scuffing our feet on the carpet). It's harmless, but startling. Like all training tools, *ScatMats* work well for some pups but not for others.

Now, you might decide to let your pup on the furniture IF you're sitting there and IF you **invite** him up by patting the sofa and saying, "Okay." Or if you pick him up and hold him in your lap. This teaches your pup to wait for your permission. That's good.

You also need to be the one who tells him when it's time to get... "Off." Combine it with a gentle waving motion of your hand and make sure he gets off, even if you have to guide him by the collar.

You can also use **Off** when your pup is **usually** allowed on the furniture, but you want him to stay off temporarily.

For example, you might have a guest who isn't comfortable with your pup sitting on the couch beside him. Or perhaps you're sitting on the couch with a plate of food on your lap. Or perhaps you're lying on the couch because you're sick.

Because he is usually allowed up there, he would be confused if he tried to jump up and you suddenly told him "No." You need a different word—one that means "Sorry, little guy, but the couch is off limits right now."

As an example, my dog Buffy lies on the couch with us when we're watching TV. But when food appears, she is not allowed to remain there. We've been so consistent in telling her "Off" when food appears that she now jumps off on her own as soon as she sees a dinner plate in our hands.

Patterns, patterns, patterns! Dogs love 'em.

Chapter 22

Stop Over-Dependency and Demanding Behaviors

Another common problem in misbehaving pups is their view that **being petted** is a right that they can demand at will.

"Jake, stop pestering me!" Kathy was sitting on the sofa trying to read. She had been petting her dog, but after a while she just wanted to read. Jake shouldered himself between her knees and wedged his head into her lap. Kathy pushed him away, but he wagged his tail and came charging right back.

Don't pet your puppy every time he solicits it.

Soliciting means nudging or mouthing your hand, pushing himself against you, or pawing at you. Now, every pup occasionally solicits petting. That's normal.

But when it happens multiple times a day, it crosses the line into being demanding, especially if the pup has other behavior issues. In other words, it's harder to stop **other** issues when you're allowing demanding behaviors.

Stay in control of soliciting behavior. Send a pushy pup to his *Place* (Chapter 16). Wait 5 minutes, then tell him to *Come* (Chapter 18) and *Sit* (Chapter 31). Then pet him. Now your petting becomes his reward for following **your** commands rather than your following **his** command of "Nudge nudge nudge, I insist that you pet me right now." It's another subtle leadership thing.

YOU should decide when to stop petting.

Suppose you're sitting on the couch watching TV. You invite your puppy up to be petted.

After 15 seconds (yes, **seconds**...not minutes) of pet-ting, tell him, "That's enough" or "All done" or "No more" (choose a phrase and stick to it). Take your hand away.

If he settles down and goes to sleep, good. But if he nudges for more petting, repeat your phrase and put him on the floor. Go on watching TV.

If he persists in seeking attention, send him to his *Place*. Or put him in his crate or ex-pen. Don't pet him or speak to him as you do so. Simply lead him into his crate or pen, and close the door.

Finally, don't hold or pet your pup *too much.*

In my experience, most pups with behavior issues are being petted and fondled too much. Ten or fifteen seconds of sincere affection and soft happy talk is plenty at any given time.

If you hold your dog too much, or sit on the couch absently stroking him while you watch TV or read a book...

You're promoting an unhealthy dependency.

Some dependent pups become so accustomed to fondling and cud-dling that they don't know how to face the world without your hand resting on their back.

When you leave them alone, they experience a form of *separation anxiety* in which they become nervous, even frantic. They might vent their anxiety by barking, digging holes in cushions, or ripping off your baseboards. Entire rooms have been destroyed by pups with dependency-based separation anxiety.

 Making your puppy dependent on being held and stroked is really awful for his mental and emotional health.

Some dependent pups become *resource guarders*. Remember we talked about resource guarding in Chapter 20. A dependent dog might growl when another person or pet approaches "his" (your) lap or "his" (your) hand.

Please don't post a video on YouTube of your dog sitting on your lap and pitching a fit at your significant other who's pretending to snuggle with you. The dog is not protecting you or showing how much he loves you. He's claiming and guarding a **resource** (your lap and hand).

"No. Off." is what you should say and onto the floor he should go and not be allowed back up.

 Dependency and resource guarding aren't funny or cute. They're psychologically unhealthy and stressful for your dog and you need to stop them before the dog becomes truly nasty or neurotic.

How do dogs like to be petted?

Every dog is different, but most dogs enjoy it when:

 You scratch their chest and between their front legs.

You rub the base of their ears. Some pups have a favorite ear, while others enjoy both ears in an alternating pattern.

You scratch atop their hindquarters at the base of their tail, which is a deliciously ticklish spot for many pups, who might respond by quivering their skin, or stretching their body, or even tapping a hind leg up and down.

 You rub their belly. Some might even sprawl on their back with a rapturous expression on their face. Other pups find this position too vulnerable and are reluctant to allow belly rubs.

How do dogs NOT like to be petted?

- Most dogs don't like being **patted** on their head. *Pat-pat-pat* feels jarring and impersonal. People who don't know much about dogs, or who don't like dogs all that much, tend to **pat** them.

  Toy dogs especially are apt to shy away from a giant hand that descends from the sky toward their vulnerable little head. Before you let strangers pet your toy dog, show them how to scratch their fingers on the pup's chest or under the chin rather than patting the head.

- Most dogs don't enjoy being hugged. They usually tolerate it, but they don't like feeling wrapped up. Especially don't let a **child** hug a dog. A common cause of dog bites is the child wrapping her arms around the dog's neck—70% of dog bites to a child under the age of 10 are bites to the face.

- Don't kiss a dog. Dogs view a kiss as a "face lick," which in the canine world is done **BY** followers **TO** leaders. So if you kiss a dog, he's more likely to see you as a follower instead of a leader.

On the other hand, it's okay for **him** to give **you** kisses, if you don't mind them.

Again though, be wary of letting small children put their faces near a dog's mouth "to be kissed." Remember that awful 70% bites-to-the-face statistic.

Chapter 23

Stop Mouthing/Biting of Your Hands

This chapter is for *mouthy puppies* who are mouthing or nipping at you from excitement.

This chapter is NOT for adolescent dogs who are growling, snapping, or threatening to bite when you do something with them that they don't like. See Chapter 44 for those dogs.

Why pups nip and bite

- Puppies naturally use their mouths to explore the world. They mouth and chew things to acquire information about that object. You need to teach the puppy that he may not do this with human hands.

- Puppies also use their mouths to play with their littermates. When they join a human family, they may not yet realize that the humans are not littermates.

- Puppies with a strong *prey instinct* use their teeth more than pups with a weak prey instinct. *Prey instinct* is an inherited compulsion to chase and bite at things that move…a running squirrel, a rolling ball, or your hands and feet. Some breeds have stronger prey instincts than others.

- Puppies who were removed from their mother and siblings too early (before 7 weeks old) tend to bite more. This is because a puppy's mother and siblings teach him something very important called **bite inhibition.**

  It works like this: If a puppy bites too hard during play, his mother or sibling will react dramatically, pouncing on the puppy and giving him a good shake or retaliatory bite. If the puppy responds properly to this chastisement by acting contrite, basically saying with his body language: "I'm sorry!" then Mother or Sibling will be satisfied that they have gotten their message across.

> In this way, a pup learns to inhibit his biting, to respect other living creatures, and to respond properly to the *social signals* of dominance and submission. A puppy removed from his mother and siblings before 7 weeks old didn't receive the full benefit of those vital lessons. These pups often end up being mouthy, resistant to correction, or pushy toward other dogs.

- Puppies from pet shops often nip and bite more because pet shop employees allowed them to be played with by prospective customers who handled the puppy inappropriately and encouraged him to roughhouse and nip.

Techniques to stop the biting

Whatever the cause, you need to control the biting now, before the puppy is older and it gets much worse.

First, two things you shouldn't do...

- **Don't jerk your hand away from the puppy's mouth.** Moving your hand simulates a prey animal trying to escape, which can trigger the pup's instinct to grab even harder.

- **Don't try to "distract" the puppy by giving him a treat or toy.** This only rewards him for biting and he will be more inclined to repeat that behavior.

Here are the things you SHOULD try:

 Return the puppy's bite with a mild "bite" of your own. As he closes his mouth around your hand, leave your hand where it is (I know...those teeth are sharp!) Say "AH-ah" and wrap the fingers of that hand around his lower jaw.

Basically this says, "Okay, you wanted my hand in your mouth, so here it is." Usually a pup quickly decides that this isn't what he signed up for! When he tries to spit out your hand, let go. Most puppies will look chagrined at that point.

 A similar technique is to keep your *thumb* inside the puppy's mouth. There is a slight indentation inside his mouth, just behind his lower front teeth, under his tongue. If Puppy closes his mouth on your hand, press down gently with your thumb. When he tries to spit out your hand, let go.

You can also use one of the **water spray** or **sudden sound** devices I mentioned in Chapter 5. With a biting puppy, it's difficult for you to activate these tools yourself, but your spouse can do it. Timing is important. Say "No" or "AH-ah" AS Puppy is biting, then spray the water or activate the sound device.

 Another technique is a **leash correction.** Grasp the leash about 6–12 inches from the pup's collar and lower your hand to the same height off the floor as his collar is. Give a quick tug on the leash directly sideways from his collar and parallel to the ground, just enough to make him let go and reconsider his biting.

If Puppy is still biting, you have not yet made your correction outweigh the reward (the fun) he's getting from the behavior.

 For these determined pups, try this— as he closes his teeth on your hand, say sharply, "AH-ah!" and use your index finger to give a stern poke on his shoulder.

When a young puppy joins your family, it's natural for him to interact with you in the only way he knows how—with his mouth. But although it's natural, you can't let it continue, or the puppy will continue believing that humans are littermates. That will lead to a lot more trouble down the line.

If the puppy is biting the kids

Well, we need to look at how this can be happening. If he's in a crate or pen, he can't chase or bite the kids

If he has his leash on, then yes, he could be mouthing or biting the kids, but then you'll have no problem administering a leash correction or activating the water spray or sound device.

You should also consider the behavior of the children. Sometimes owners have unrealistic expectations that a young puppy is supposed to play gently even when the kids are running around and inciting him to play roughly. Children shouldn't be roughhousing or wrestling with the puppy.

If a child is too young to understand how to play gently, or if the child is older but refuses to follow your rules, you should remove the pup (or the child) from the situation.

Chapter 24

Stop Barking

In Chapter 13, I explained how to handle barking in the crate or ex-pen. That's always a no-no, so you say "No" or "AH-ah" and follow up with a corrective technique.

Barking **outside** of the crate and pen is handled pretty much the same way—except there are some valid reasons for barking outside of the crate and pen.

Many dogs will bark when they hear a strange sound or see something out of the ordinary. You don't want to stop your dog from being a good watchdog.

But most dogs bark far too much, making them useless as watchdogs. They're like *The Boy Who Cried Wolf.* No one even checks to see what they're barking at anymore. Frequent barking also keeps a dog in a heightened state of excitability instead of calmness.

So be honest—is your pup...

- barking at the neighbors?
- barking at the neighbor's dog?
- barking at passersby on the sidewalk?
- barking at kids on bicycles?
- barking at the mailman?

- barking at the garbage truck and UPS truck?
- barking when other neighborhood dogs bark?

Our dogs need to be taught to recognize familiar things that are harmless. The way they learn to do this is by **US** telling them.

For example, your pup looks out the window and sees an ax murderer on the sidewalk. He starts barking. You look out and see…the sweet old lady from Apartment 2A shuffling along with her walker.

She's harmless. You don't want your pup barking at that lady. So stop it with **No,** plus a corrective technique (Chapter 5). The message is: "Don't bark at that person or situation. At all."

You're telling your puppy that as you, as the leader, have evaluated that person or situation and declared him/her/it harmless. That's what leaders do and a respectful dog should accept your judgment.

Now suppose a delivery man is standing on your porch. It's perfectly fine for your pup to bark—a few times. Then use the phrase you learned in Chapter 22: "That's enough" or "All done" or "No more." Some owners add "Stop" because it's such a natural word when you want him to stop barking.

Wait 2 seconds and if he hasn't stopped, use one of the corrective techniques from Chapter 5.

You want your pup to learn that yes, barking at someone on the porch is okay, **but when you say stop, it needs to stop.** He needs to accept that **YOU** will take over and handle the situation. That's what leaders do.

Barking when the doorbell rings

...or when someone knocks at the door. See Chapter 26.

Barking when you're not home

This is bad for the neighbors and bad for the dog's state of mind. Some owners aren't even aware of how much their pup barks when they're not home. It's a good idea to leave the house sometimes and lurk outside for 10 or 15 minutes, listening.

Here are some tips for stopping this problem:

 Block his view of the outdoors. Leave him in a room with no view outside, or else install shades or drapes to block his view.

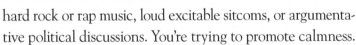

 Block sounds from outdoors. Put on soothing music—classical, soft jazz, elevator music, or nature sounds. Or tune the TV to the Golf Channel. No hard rock or rap music, loud excitable sitcoms, or argumentative political discussions. You're trying to promote calmness.

 Provide more exercise and interesting activities. Tired pups are more likely to sleep. People often think their dog gets plenty of exercise wandering around the yard. Unless your dog is tiny, that's seldom true. If a pup doesn't have anything interesting to do, he will feel bored and frustrated, and pups express boredom and frustration by destroying things or barking.

 Discourage clingy behaviors. Reread Chapter 22. Your puppy needs to learn to stand on his own four feet without you frequently holding him or cuddling with him.

 Stage corrective set-ups. This means leaving the house, lurking close by until you hear barking, then coming back inside (perhaps sneaking in a back door) to correct him. Alternatively, you can leave while your spouse remains hidden inside, listening and prepared to emerge and correct.

 Get your dog a companion...but not yet. If your dog absolutely must be alone for more than four hours a day, consider getting a second dog to keep him company. But not now! Don't try to raise two new dogs *at the same time*. They will tend to bond with each other and follow each other rather than you. Then you'll have **two** barkers.

Instead, work with the puppy you have, and when he is well-behaved, respectful, and 100% housebroken, then look for another dog to keep the first one company during those long lonely hours. I recommend adopting an adult dog of the opposite sex. Definitely not a puppy if you're gone all day!

How to leave your pup home alone

How you leave the house can make a big difference in how your pup acts when you're gone. For example, don't do this...

"Jake sweetie, Mummy and Daddy have to go out for awhile, okay? We're sorry to leave you all by yourself. But we have to, Jake. Don't be mad and don't be scared. We'll come back. It will be all right, don't worry, we'll be home soon!"

Ugh! When you need to leave your puppy alone, don't make a big emotional scene. A melodramatic exit revs up your pup's nervous system and creates anxiety, which he will probably try to relieve through chewing, digging, or barking.

Instead:

1. Provide an activity/play session before you leave.

2. Just before you leave, take him outside one last time to relieve himself.

3. Turn on soothing music or a relaxing TV station like the Golf Channel. Put him in his crate or pen or gated room. Give him a Kong toy to chew on.

4. Sit for a few minutes, reading the paper or watching TV. Then say calmly, "Bye, Jake. Be a good boy." No fondling, emotional farewells, or lingering looks. Just leave.

How to come home to your puppy

Similarly, when you come home, don't burst in the door and overwhelm your pup with hugs and kisses.

After many quiet hours alone, a melodramatic entrance is too stimulating for your puppy's nervous system. He will begin to anticipate your homecoming long before you arrive, and as he awaits the big emotional scene, he will become more anxious and revved up.

Instead:

1. Come in. Say, "Hi, Jake." **Then ignore him.** Hang up your jacket. Don't pay any attention to your puppy. Don't even look at him. A few welcoming barks are fine, but if he makes a racket, correct it (Chapter 13).

2. Soon he should be calmer and more settled. If he is in a crate or pen, open the crate door. Remember to have him "Wait" inside the crate until you say "Okay." Cue him, "Do you need to go OUT?" and take him directly outside to the bathroom.

If your pup is barking outdoors

A dog should not be outside by himself. Someone should be out with him to make sure he doesn't eat something he shouldn't, or find a way to escape, or dig holes in your flower bed, or bark.

When you're outside with him, you can both monitor his safety and correct unwanted behaviors, including barking.

Be prepared to deal with any problems by keeping him on a long line (15 to 30 feet long), either holding it or letting him drag it so you can easily get hold of him if he starts barking at a neighbor.

Usually one of the corrective techniques from Chapter 5 will suffice for outdoor barking. This is especially true when you've already taught the puppy the meaning of "No" or "AH-ah" and he respects you as the leader.

This is one of the great benefits of teaching "No"—you can stop unwanted behaviors so easily.

But I wanted an outdoor dog!

Were you hoping your dog could *stay* outdoors by himself during the day? While you went off to work and the kids to school?

You shouldn't risk disturbing the peace of your neighbors.

Even a dedicated dog lover like myself becomes frustrated and angry when an owner puts a dog outside and trots off to work, leaving the rest of us listening to barking.

In fact, I'm the first one on the phone to my homeowners association, animal control, and the police.

Neighbors who are **not** dedicated dog lovers may resort to a BB gun, rat poison, transporting your pup to a distant city, or opening your gate so your nuisance dog "escapes."

In addition, outdoor dogs are not happy.

If you live on a 20-acre farm and your livestock guardian dog is guarding your sheep...or if you live in Alaska and your sled dogs are pulling sleds...or if you live out in the rural countryside and take your pack of hounds hunting every weekend...

> ...those dogs are fine with living outdoors because they're regularly performing the work they are genetically hard-wired to do. They're willing to give up family life in order to "follow their genes" and *work.*

> But if you want a dog as a family companion, only an indoor dog can fulfill this role. Remember, dogs are sociable creatures who want to live *among* their family.

Your pup wants to be in the same room with you, listening to your conversations and lying on the rug near you as you watch TV.

Dogs who spend hours and hours outdoors are forced to live "outside" their pack, on the fringes of it, not immersed in day-to-day family life.

So please, bring your dog indoors and start teaching calmness (Chapter 9), housebreaking (Chapter 34), and so on. Your dog will be a fine *indoor* companion if you follow the book faithfully.

Your neighbors will appreciate it too.

Chapter 25

Stop Jumping on People

Jumping on people looks cute when a pup is 3 months old, but it becomes such a serious behavior problem that you shouldn't allow jumping even in a young puppy.

A jumping dog:

- tears clothing

- leaves dirty footprints on clothing

- scratches people with sharp toenails

- nips people, even accidentally from excitement

- makes children and frail people stumble or fall

Along with the damage that can be done to people, **jumping creates an overexcited mind-set in the dog,** which is the very opposite of the *calm* mind-set we're trying to teach.

Even a normally active dog feels more secure when he's in a calm, relaxed state of mind.

Perhaps you're thinking, "But my dog only jumps on *me,* not on other people."

Even so, he's still practicing an excitable mind-set that is psychologically stressful. And God forbid, if anything happened to you and your pup needed to be re-homed, fewer people will adopt a jumping dog.

So you really should stop this behavior as soon as it starts. It's not safe or considerate of other people. And it's definitely not good for your puppy's all-important state of mind.

Don't try to stop jumping with these techniques.

Don't put your hands on a jumping dog. Not even to push him off. Because YOU might think you're pushing him off, but HE often views it as *petting* or *fondling.* From his perspective, those consequences are *positive.* He's getting attention and petting when he jumps. So keep your hands off him.

Don't turn your back on a jumping dog. That only teaches your puppy that he needs to sneak around to the front before he jumps. Some pups don't even do that—they're just as happy to jump against your backside and knock you forward.

Three effective corrections for jumping

The first technique to extinguish jumping is a knee raise. **AS** the pup starts his jump, raise one knee as though you were doing a high-step march in a parade. A larger dog will bump against your raised knee, while a smaller dog will bump against your raised shin, ankle, or foot.

You want him to conclude, "Hmm, that wasn't the outcome I was hoping for. An uncomfortable *bump* and I didn't even get petted!"

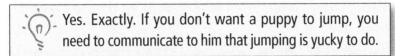 Yes. Exactly. If you don't want a puppy to jump, you need to communicate to him that jumping is yucky to do.

Don't make eye contact as you raise your knee. Eye contact is positive attention that jumping pups seek. Just watch him out of the corner of your eye so you'll be ready with another knee raise in case he tries a second jump.

Only when he has settled down (wait a good 10 seconds) should you look at him and acknowledge him. In a calm voice, say, "Hello, Jake." If he takes that as encouragement to jump, repeat your knee raise and this time wait a little longer before acknowledging him. You want him to learn this pattern: "jump → yucky bump + no attention."

The second technique to extinguish jumping is a sideways *tug* of the leash. If you remember from Chapter 9, a puppy with any behavior problems should be on a leash in your house. Jumping is definitely a behavior problem.

Grasp the leash about a foot from his collar, move your hand toward the jumping dog (to create a little slack) and then sideways and parallel to the ground.

For a sensitive puppy, the movement of the leash can be just a pull that puts him off-balance. For a determined jumper, it should be more of a "popping" tug that gets his attention and provides a negative consequence to the jumping.

The third technique to extinguish jumping is to startle the pup in the act of jumping. Being startled is a negative consequence to some (but definitely not all) pups. Try a spray of water, a shrill sound from the *Barker Breaker,* or a puff of air from the *Pet Convincer* or *Pet Corrector.*

The difficulty here is that you need to have the device in your hand when the pup jumps. So you should stage a **set-up** in which you hold the device behind your back out of his sight. Then "present yourself" to your puppy in a way that might cause him to jump.

Don't pat your leg or your chest trying to **goad** him into jumping— that wouldn't be fair.

But certainly you can play with him, then stand still facing him, with one arm hanging naturally at your side and the other hand behind your back. If he jumps, spray the water or activate the device. Some pups will veer away and not want to repeat the jump.

What if your puppy jumps on other people?

You might have helpful friends who would be willing to do the knee-raise technique. But you can't count on all your guests doing that. Think of Uncle Henry with his arthritis. Or your 4-year-old niece. No, **YOU** should be the one to correct your puppy for jumping on other people.

Until this problem is solved, a jumping puppy should be on a leash whenever other people are around.

Either you're holding the leash or he's dragging it. Then you can quickly gain control and administer the appropriate degree of tug if he jumps on anyone. Remember, a gentle tug for very young or sensitive pups, a firmer tug for more determined pups.

Alternatively, if your pup is deterred by a spray of water, sound device, or puffed air device, keep them close at hand.

> One of the most valuable lessons you can teach your puppy is that he will be rewarded for calmness and corrected for excitability. This state of mind will stay with him throughout his life, which is exactly what you want in a great family dog.

Chapter 26

Take Charge of the Doorbell

When someone comes to the door, do you need to grab at your puppy and try to shush him while you're trying to open the door?

Do you find yourself trying to read your visitor's lips over the racket your pup is making?

If your puppy keeps barking or lunging at people even after you've answered the door...

- he is either barking mindlessly, with no self-control

- OR he is taking it upon himself to decide whether your visitor is a threat, when he should be leaving that decision up to the leader...which is supposed to be you.

Either way, this is not the behavior or attitude you want.

Once your pup has sounded the alarm, he should turn the situation over to you. If **YOU** decide the person at the door is harmless, your pup should accept your judgment and be quiet.

Teach your pup to be civilized when the doorbell rings.

YOU should answer the doorbell—not your puppy. Certainly he can accompany you, but he should not be in front of you. You want him to feel confident that **YOU** are the one who will face potential "threats" at the door. That's a leader's job.

You'll need a friend to help you. In fact, several friends would be better—though not all at once!

Here's the set-up. You sit on the sofa pretending to watch TV. Your puppy is lying down or sitting or standing near you. Of course, he's on leash, yes? A pup who isn't responding to the doorbell properly has a behavior issue, which means he shouldn't be off leash inside the house.

The doorbell rings. You've already told your friend to ring *just once,* no matter how long it takes you to open the door.

Your pup launches into action, leaping up and rushing for the door. He's attached to the leash, so he can't get very far, but he gives it his best shot, scrabbling across the floor, pulling the leash taut and probably barking up a storm.

We don't want any of that.

So if your pup is in front of you, stop. Don't take another step toward the door.

Use the leash-handling techniques *(Loosen-Tug)* you learned in Chapter 11 to get your puppy to a position beside you and slightly behind you. Then loosen the leash so the clip hangs straight down and there is a U-shape in the leash.

Repeat and repeat and repeat, making each tug firmer than the previous one until finally he chooses to stay beside or behind you on a loose leash.

If he's too strong for you, he needs a different collar (Chapter 11).

Once you have him under control while you're standing still, you'll probably find that the barking has stopped too. If not, correct the barking with the techniques from Chapter 5.

Now take one step toward the door. If he rushes again, stop and repeat your leash-handling technique. (Hopefully you've chosen a patient friend and explained that it might be a while before you actually open the door!)

Eventually, you should be able to reach the door with your pup walking beside/behind you like a good *follower* dog.

Now open the door. If he tries to rush past you, don't hold him back with the leash. He won't learn anything that way. Instead, do your **Loosen-Tug** technique. If he keeps ignoring it, he needs a different collar.

And if your puppy JUMPS on the person when you let them in? Oh, you already know how to handle that (Chapter 25)!

Chapter 27

Make Your Pup Move

I use a handy word to tell my pup to *be somewhere else.* Some owners say "Shoo" while others prefer "Go on" or "Move." When I was growing up in New England, the expression we used was "Go on, get." An odd expression, but it worked well enough!

There are no tricks to teaching this. Combine the new sound with a natural shooing motion of your hand and *spatial pressure* (discussed in Chapter 15)—whatever it takes to make your pup move away. When he does so, praise.

It's a handy word. In fact, when it fits the situation, it comes quickly to mind as the perfect word.

- Dog standing in a flower bed. "Shoo!"

- Dog lying across the doorway blocking you when you're carrying plates of food into the dining room. "Move."

- Dog wandering into the garage where you're repairing the lawnmower, with sharp tools lying around. "Go on."

- Dog poking his head into the bedroom. You and your spouse are engaged in...um..."Hey, go on, get!" As I said, it comes quickly to mind when it fits the situation.

Chapter 28

"Leave It"

Along with "No" and "AH-ah", there's another phrase you can use when you don't want your puppy to do something.

No, you're not going to "break his spirit" by telling him that he can't do things.

In fact, whenever we show a pup that he *shouldn't* do something, we also show him (or he figures out) what he *should* do instead.

- We teach him that he *shouldn't* pull on the leash, that instead he *should* walk with the leash loose.

- We teach him that he *shouldn't* bark in the crate, that instead he *should* be quiet and relaxed.

- We teach him that he *shouldn't* rush through doors ahead of us, that instead he *should* wait until we give him permission to go through.

Dogs understand this concept perfectly—do this, not that. You're not hurting your puppy's feelings or harming your relationship with him by teaching him what he should and shouldn't do. Won't happen. So what is this new phrase to tell your pup not to do something?

"Leave it" or "Don't touch"

Use this phrase to tell your pup that something is off limits or that you want him to come away from something that interests him. For example...

- You're on a walk and he spots a bag of spilled chips on the ground. "Leave it!" is the perfect command here.

- You're walking with him in a pet store. He stops to sniff at a display stand where other dogs have probably left their urinary "calling card." You decide that you want him away from there before he gets any ideas! "Leave it."

- You bring home a hamster in a cage. When your puppy approaches the cage, sniffing, you say, "Leave it." You want him to back off and look up at you, showing by his respectful body language that he understands.

Teaching "Leave it"

1. Put your puppy on leash and place his favorite treat on the floor. Make sure he sees it, then put your foot over it so it's covered by your shoe.

2. Say, "Leave it." If he sniffs or licks or paws at your shoe, say, "AH-ah" and use the leash to guide him away. Be gentle. He doesn't yet know what you want.

3. When you've moved him away from the treat, loosen the leash. If he goes after it again, repeat your "AH-ah" and leash guidance. If he persists and persists and won't quit, increase to a sharper tug or switch to some other corrective technique (Chapter 5) that you know works for him.

4. When he is no longer going after the treat, tell him "Good boy." Pick up the treat and put it in your pocket. Take a break, play a game with him or something, then repeat the exercise. You can use different kinds of tempting treats, if you have them.

5. You want him to learn that when you say "Leave it," he must not pursue something any further, even if he would love to have it.

6. After a good number of repetitions, place the treat on the floor and say, "Leave it" but don't cover it with your foot. Just be ready! If he goes after it, be quick with your "AH-ah!" and get your shoe over it! Again, do as many repetitions as necessary until he no longer goes after the treat even when it's in plain sight.

7. Next, hold the treat in your hand. Say, "Leave it" and bend over until your hand is only a few inches off the floor. Drop the treat onto the floor. Be ready to block the puppy and protect the treat with your shoe, if necessary.

8. The next step is to say, "Leave it" and toss the treat a few feet away from the dog, being prepared to block him or check him with the leash, if necessary.

9. When he's doing well indoors, practice in your backyard. First go outside without your pup and place some tempting treats or toys in different parts of the yard. Then with your puppy on leash, meander around the yard. When he notices one of your "planted" items, say "Leave it" in a firm voice.

> Timing is very important. You want to say "Leave it" **the moment your pup "locks onto"** or makes his first move toward a treat or toy. If you're too slow and he's already lunging after it, it will be much harder for him to stop.

Chapter 29

Take Charge of the Toys

Is your floor littered with lots of dog toys? A tennis ball here. Two chew bones over there. A plush teddy bear on the sofa. Squeaky toys on the rug by the door. Is that okay?

Sure, IF your puppy...

 is NOT a destructive chewer,

 is respectful of you and your family, and

 has no behavior issues.

But to maintain interest, I recommend rotating toys. Let your pup have a few toys for a few weeks. Then put them away and offer a different set.

Rotating toys keeps your pup's mind open to accepting new things, which is a healthy attitude. Rotating toys also makes them seem new and exciting whenever you return them.

But if your puppy is a destructive chewer, he should *NOT* have a bunch of toys.

When the floor is littered with toys, a destructive pup might assume that *everything* is chewable, including your belongings.

I give a destructive chewer only one or two toys, as tough and durable as possible. Later in this chapter, I'll recommend toys.

Having only two toys makes it clear to a destructive dog that those two objects are the only things he is allowed to chew on.

Everything else he tries to pick up receives an "AH-ah!" or "Leave it!" (Chapter 28)

The good news is that most destructive chewers grow out of the habit with maturity. So at some point, you should be able to add more toys and begin rotating them for variety.

A pup with behavior issues should *NOT* have a bunch of toys.

Just as pups with behavior issues tend to be sleeping on their owners' beds and furniture, they usually also have free access to toys, either scattered on the floor or in a dog-accessible toy box.

This presents us with a great opportunity! You see, along with sleeping spots (Chapter 21) and food (Chapter 20), *toys* are a valuable resource to your puppy.

> Therefore, one of the best ways to establish the proper leader-follower relationship with a pup who is being disrespectful or pushy or is *acting out* in some way, is for you to **control the toys**.

With these pups, don't leave toys down all day and don't offer free access to a toy box. Free access to toys can create a dog who feels entitled.

Instead, you want this pup to understand that toys are *privileges* controlled by you. Make sure he watches you as you select *one* toy from YOUR toy shelf, which is not dog-accessible. Have him *Sit,* then hand it to him. After a short session of playing with that toy, make sure he watches you pick it up and put it back on YOUR shelf. This simple routine is a very big thing to dogs!

Pups who are possessive of their toys

In Chapter 20, we talked about *resource guarding,* which is a dangerous behavior problem. It typically starts with a dog hovering over something (a toy, his food, your lap) and growling when someone approaches or extends their hand toward it. Usually it gets worse and worse until the dog finally bites.

At the first sign of possessiveness, take that toy away as soon as you can do so safely. Put it away in a drawer. A few days later, try a different toy. If he does the same thing, pick up every single toy for a full month while you continue implementing all of the chapters of this book.

If you reach a point where you think you've been successful in establishing the proper leader-follower relationship, you can try reintroducing *one* toy and see what happens.

Chapter 30

Games NOT to Play with Your Puppy

I don't recommend wrestling games.

- If you use your hands to playfully wrestle with your pup, you're encouraging him to mouth and nip at your hands.

- Wrestling games also teach him to resist and struggle when you try to roll him onto his side or back. Those positions are important for grooming and health care. You don't want him resisting those positions.

I don't recommend chase games.

It can seem like great fun to creep toward your puppy with your hands outstretched like claws, whispering in an ominous tone, "I'm…gonna…GET YOU!"

Or when you stamp your foot and make a teasing lunge toward him, and he woofs in alarm and dashes away. Upload it to YouTube and watch the Likes pour in!

Unfortunately, chasing games are not good for your relationship with your puppy. What you're doing is teaching him that when you reach for him, he should run away from you. In fact, he can quite easily evade you, which you definitely don't want him to learn.

 What if your PUP is the one doing the chasing? Should you encourage your puppy to chase after YOU?

Well, that depends…

- If he is otherwise well-behaved, and he just lopes playfully after you without nipping or jumping, and if when you stop running, he settles down quickly…fine.

- But if he gets so excited that he nips or jumps, or shoves his body against your legs, or tangles up your feet, you don't want to encourage that kind of behavior.

Some pups simply can't engage in chase games in a civilized manner. Often these are pups with a strong *prey instinct* that compels them to chase and grab at things that move.

> **Young children should not play chase games with a dog.** Young children can't judge when a dog's behavior is over the line, and they can't correct a dog with enough authority. For safety's sake, don't allow your dog to chase any child, and don't allow your kids to run away from your dog.

Summary: There are much better games than wrestling and chase to play with your puppy. In my book, *Teach Your Dog 100 English Words*, I cover great games such as *Fetch, Hide and Seek, Find it,* and (for some dogs) *Tug.*

Chapter 31

Sit and Stay

Some owners will say, "I've already taught my pup to sit." But when I ask for a demonstration, I hear this...

"Sit, Charlie. Sit down. Come on, Charlie, sit. Sit! Charlie?"

At this point the frustrated owner usually holds up a treat. Then Charlie sits.

Remember that pups learn from patterns and consequences. Charlie's owner had taught her puppy that it's okay to just stand there or fool around while she spews out a bunch of sounds. In the end, he always gets the treat anyway, so why rush?

Let's instead teach your puppy that he will hear **one** *Sit* sound, then he will sit, either on his own or with help.

 And then—very important, this—he must ***remain*** sitting until given permission to get up.

Why is that important? Because *Sit* is a controlled position, which might be why you told him to sit in the first place.

For example, you're at the vet and you want Charlie to sit so the vet can examine his eyes. After 3 or 4 commands, Charlie finally touches his bottom to the floor. But then he immediately stands up again. The vet doesn't find this very helpful.

What you want is for *Sit* to mean, "Plunk your bottom on the floor and keep it there until I tell you otherwise."

Sit is a marvelous control word that puts your pup in an accessible position for examining, grooming, or attaching the leash.

Sit also gives your puppy a way to say "Please" or "Thanks." For example, I have my dogs give me a polite sit before I put their food bowls on the floor or attach their leashes for a walk.

So even if you think your puppy already knows how to *Sit*, it's worthwhile to teach him to sit on **one** command and to remain sitting until you release him with "Okay." This is very do-able!

Teach Sit by luring with food

Don't worry, we're going to phase out the food. But if your puppy is motivated by food, it can be a good way to start.

With your pup on leash and standing more or less in front of you, say, "Sit." **Say it only once.** Pronounce that "t" at the end: *siT*. Your voice shouldn't go UP at the end. Don't ask "Sit??"

Move a tasty treat toward his nose. But before it gets there, lift it a little higher as you keep it moving *slowly* up and over his muzzle, up and over his eyes, and up between his ears.

To keep his eyes on the treat as it moves up over his head, your pup needs to bend his neck back. But because his neck can't bend far when he's standing, many puppies will drop their hindquarters into a sitting position so they can see better.

It takes some practice to get the trajectory of the moving treat just right. Don't hold it too high, else he'll jump for it!

If he didn't drop into a sit on his own, pull slightly upward and backward with the leash, just a little bit. Often that will be enough to nudge him into a sit. If not, use your other hand to push down on his hindquarters (just behind his two hipbones, near his tail). Don't push down on his back.

> Whatever it took to get him sitting, say "Yes" or "Good" and then give him the treat. It's okay if he doesn't remain sitting. We'll work on that soon.

Phase out the food

After many repetitions where you lure the puppy into a *Sit* with food and/or the leash and/or your hands…it's time to phase out the food lure. Don't show him any food at all—keep it hidden in your pocket.

Say "Sit" and add the familiar hand motion just over his head (but with no food). If he sits, say "Yes" or "Good" and **then** reach into your pocket and pull out the treat.

Command → behavior → praise → reach for the treat

Now you can phase out the treats by progressing from **constant** treating (every time) to **variable** treating (every other time, or every 3rd time) to **random** treating (only occasionally).

Remember, if your pup doesn't sit on one command, don't repeat it. Just *place* him into a Sit with a leash tug or your hands.

If he's persistent about not sitting on his own, make your leash tug more firm. You want him to conclude that sitting on his own is much more comfortable than being "helped."

Teach your puppy to STAY sitting...basic

Once your puppy is reliably sitting on one command, start requiring him to HOLD the sit.

Get him sitting beside you so you're both facing the same direction. Shorten the leash by folding most of it into your hand so there's only a short length of leash between his collar and your hand.

> Yes, usually you want a very loose leash with a big loop in it. But for this exercise, a short leash is better.

Then just stand there. He's supposed to just sit there.

If he tries to stand up or lie down, *check* him with the leash. That means quickly moving the leash in whichever direction will prevent him from standing or lying down. You might need to move it backward, or upward, or to the left or right. It's easier to check him when the leash is pretty short.

If you weren't quite fast enough and he gets all the way up, use the leash (and your hands if necessary) to reposition him in the sitting position. Don't repeat the word.

At first, have him stay sitting for just 5 seconds. Then say, "Okay" and encourage him to get up and move around. Gradually increase to 15 and then 30 seconds. Yup, it's boring when you're both doing nothing, but that's about to change!

Teach your puppy to STAY sitting...intermediate

So far you've been teaching your puppy that "Sit" means sitting and staying there until you say "Okay."

So it isn't absolutely necessary to add the word "Stay."

But "Stay" is such a natural word to use when we want a dog to stay put, isn't it? We end up saying it anyway, so I usually just go ahead and teach it.

Now, I don't say it when I'm standing right beside my dog. As we've been teaching him, "Sit" *does* mean to sit and to stay sitting. How hard is that, really? I mean, I'm standing right there beside him!

But when I start moving away from my dog, especially outdoors or in a distracting environment, I do like to add "Stay" as a reminder.

So here's how to teach it:

1. Get your pup sitting beside you, facing the same direction. Shorten the leash so you can check him if he tries to move.

2. Place one hand in front of his face, about 6–12 inches from his eyes, your palm open and facing him, like a cautionary stop signal. If you remember, you introduced this hand signal when you were teaching him to *Wait*.

3. At the same time as the signal, say, "Stay." Say it with confidence. Don't say "Stay?" as though you're asking him.

4. Now take a very short step in front of him and immediately pivot so you're facing him. As you do so, raise the shortened leash over his head so it's **slightly** taut. Remember how you did this when you were reminding him to stay on his *Place*.

   If he starts to stand up, say "AH-ah." Don't say "Stay." Dogs connect the sound they hear with the action they're performing at that moment. You don't want him to connect the sound *Stay* with the act (or even the thought) of moving!

   As you say "AH-ah", be quick with the leash, tightening it upward and backward (toward his hindquarters) in an attempt to check him **before** he gets all the way up. If you're too slow, just reposition him without another word. Without moving your feet, you should be able to hold his front end in position with the leash, while you reach over and push his hind end into a sit, so he's back in the same place he started.

If instead he tries to lie down, again try to check him with the leash **before** he sinks all the way down. If you're too slow, use the leash or your hands to get him back up and reposition him without a word.

5. On the first day you try this, aim for your pup to hold his Sit-Stay for 10 straight seconds. Count in your head. Each time you have to correct him, start your count again.

6. When he has held his position for 10 seconds, step back to his side. Again, as you move, use the *slightly* taut leash over his head to help him hold his position.

7. When you get back to his side, pause for 5 more seconds so he learns not to misinterpret your return as a cue to get up. If he does get up, just reposition him. Count to 5 again, then praise him calmly, "Gooood. Goood." If he gets up when you praise, just reposition him and praise calmly again.

8. Finally, when he is holding position for your praise, you can release him with a cheerful "Okay!"

9. Each day, add another 5 to 10 seconds to your count so that by the end of the week he is holding his *Sit* for about a minute while you stand right in front of him.

10. Also relax the leash so you aren't holding it over his head as a reminder to hold position. That's his responsibility now.

Don't rush your puppy! For example, don't push him to hold a Sit-Stay for a full minute on the very first day and conclude that he is a Wonder Dog who doesn't need any more practice.

PRACTICE is what makes a pup rock-solid on the Sit-Stay. Like the concert pianist who faithfully practices simple finger exercises even when he could do them in his sleep, a pup who practices lots and lots of short *Sit-Stays* will end up much better trained.

Teach your pup to STAY sitting...advanced

Can your pup do these four things?

1. Hold a Sit-Stay **for a full minute?**

2. Hold a Sit-Stay **even after you've returned to his side?**

3. Hold a Sit-Stay **even while you're praising him?**

4. Hold a Sit-Stay **until you release him with "Okay"?**

Yes? Then let's make it more interesting for both of you!

Circle around him

Instead of returning directly to his side, circle around him before stopping at his side. At first, hold the leash slightly taut above his head as you go around him, to remind him to stay put. Of course, he can turn his head to see where you're going.

Add distractions

Remember the distractions you used to "proof" your pup when he was learning *Place* (Chapter 16) and *Wait* (Chapter 15)?

Time for those distractions again! After the simple ones, try these: Have one of your kids walk by, bouncing a ball. Have one of your kids run by. Have one of your kids skip rope.

> **Don't TEASE the puppy.** Don't speak to him or even look at him. You're not trying to make him fail. You're trying to build up his confidence that he CAN hold his *Sit* even with distractions.

Increase distance

Once your pup is successful with distractions while you're standing right in front of him, move to the end of the leash and repeat the distractions.

If he breaks his Sit-Stay while you're at the end of the leash, go back to him to correct him.

Don't try to correct him from the end of the leash. You'll only end up pulling him TOWARD you.

Especially don't call out, "Stay!" when you see him starting to move. He should never hear that word when he's in the process of *moving.*

Remember not to stare at him. If you meet his eyes, he may think you're inviting him to come to you. Or he may feel uncomfortable under your scrutiny and try to avoid your gaze by lying down or walking away.

So look to the right of your pup. Look to the left. Look up and count the dust bunnies on the ceiling or the clouds in the sky. Rely on your peripheral vision to keep track of your pup.

Increase time

Go from a minute to two minutes, then three minutes. That's plenty long enough for sitting still. If you need your puppy to stay put for a longer period of time, put him on his *Place.* There he can change his positions as he chooses.

Finally, drop the leash and walk around the room

and repeat your distractions.

"What's the difference between Wait and Stay?"

WAIT means "Don't cross this boundary." You use *Wait* when you don't want your pup to go through a door or gate, or enter a room, or jump out of your car...until (and unless) you say so.

The boundary must be clear to your puppy. In other words, he must be able to **SEE** the difference between "here" and "there." For example, a physical marker such as a door frame, or gate posts. Or an obvious change of footing such as vinyl floor to carpet, or grass to concrete.

With *Wait,* as long as your puppy doesn't cross the boundary, you don't care whether he stands, sits, lies down, or wanders around on his side of the boundary. He simply can't cross it.

STAY means "Hold an exact position." If you tell him to *Sit,* he has to stay sitting. He can't lie down, or stand up, or move two feet to the right.

Stay is much stricter than **Wait.** Sometimes you need that strictness. You might want your pup to sit still so the vet can examine his teeth. In such cases, it wouldn't do for your pup to stand up and walk away, or flop onto his side.

 When you need your puppy to stay in a particular position, that's when you use *Stay.*

Chapter 32

Your Puppy Should Accept Handling of Every Part of His Body

This chapter could also be titled "Handling Your Pup Without Getting Into World War III."

Honestly, some dogs pitch a fit when their owner simply tries to examine some part of their body, or comb out mats, or brush their teeth, or clip their nails. If that doesn't sound like much fun, it isn't.

A dog who protests or grumbles or wriggles around when you open his mouth, peer into his ears, trim his nails, or try to get him to sit still so you can pull a tick off his belly...

...is second-guessing your decisions about what is best for him. He doesn't yet trust you to handle the leadership role.

That's why this chapter is so important. It's not about the actual grooming process. It's about building the right leader-follower relationship, teaching your puppy to trust you, and developing your own confidence that you can handle and control your pup—whether or not he understands **why.**

Dogs have the mental and emotional maturity of a toddler. Every parent has had to say to their toddler, "Because I said so." With toddlers and dogs, long-winded explanations get you nowhere. They need to do what you say because you are in charge of their health and well-being

and you know more than they do about what's best.

In my canine health book, *11 Things You Must Do Right To Keep Your Dog Healthy and Happy,* I show you how to actually groom your dog—brushing and bathing, cleaning his ears and teeth, and clipping his nails.

In the training book you're reading now, we focus on teaching your pup to **accept being handled,** to remain calm and quiet as you move his body into different positions and touch and feel all over his body.

"But I take my dog to a professional groomer!"

You should still do everything in this chapter.

 First, because you want your pup to have the right (respect-ful) attitude toward *you.*

 Second, because you want to be sure that you can easily handle and control your pup even when he doesn't under-stand (or like) something.

 And third, because you shouldn't turn ALL of your dog's grooming over to someone else. You should be personally inspecting his teeth, eyes, ears, and paws on a regular basis. This is how you catch health problems early when they're still readily treatable.

First, choose a handling/grooming area.

Remember that dogs learn best through routines—doing things the same way, in the same order.

So when you're teaching these handling exercises, it will help your puppy if you always go to the same place in your house. This will help him remember what happens there.

I like to use a table for handling and grooming. Pups are usually more hesitant to act up when they're on a table. It's a new experience for them, and they might be a bit concerned about falling off. So you have more control over the puppy on a table.

The downside is that if you're not very alert, a quick pup *could* actually jump or fall off.

So if you're worried about a high table, or if your puppy is large, might you have a lower table such as an old coffee table? Or can you make some other kind of raised platform? You can kneel beside a low table, or sit on a hassock or footstool or even a sturdy box.

Make sure the surface is *non-slip.* Rubber is ideal. You might use a rubber bathmat or a plush bathmat with rubber backing.

If you must use the floor, put down the same kind of mat. Unless your pup is very calm and stays still, don't do these exercises directly on a slick vinyl or wood floor.

Introduction to the sitting position

First, you're going to place your pup in a sitting position. Now you might be thinking, "My puppy already sits on command. Can't I just tell him to sit?"

Well, the goal of handling exercises is to teach your pup **to accept being handled.**

There will be times in his life when you (or the vet) will need to move his body into different positions in order to provide medical care. By getting him used to being handled and moved about, you'll be making those experiences much less stressful for him. Also for you and the vet!

So yes, even if your puppy knows how to sit, you should PLACE him in a sitting position.

There are two ways to do that:

 The Push. With your right hand, hold his collar to keep him steady. With your left hand, push down on his hindquarters (just behind his two hipbones, near his tail). Don't push down on his BACK. His spine and vertebrae are too sensitive for heavy pressure.

 The Fold. Place your right palm on his chest. Place your left hand (if he's small) or your left forearm (if he's larger) against the back of his rear legs (just above his "knees"). In one smooth motion, push his chest toward his rump while tucking his back legs forward to fold him into a sit over your hand or forearm. Don't worry, it sounds harder than it is!

Say "Sit" as you're placing him into the position. Yes, even if he already knows the word. The moment he's sitting, tell him "Good. Gooood dog." Calm voice. If you praise enthusiastically, he may get excited and try to jump around.

Keep your hands on him for a few seconds, then give him a treat and move right along to the next position.

Introduction to the standing position

1. Hook the fingers of your right hand (palm UP) in his collar under his chin.

2. Place your left hand (palm DOWN) under his stomach, way back in his groin area where his hindquarters are all bunched up as he sits there.

3. Pull his collar gently forward and lift the BACK of your left hand gently into his stomach/groin area. This should raise him to a standing position. Say "Sta-a-a-nd" (drawing the word out) as you do so.

4. Once he's standing, keep your left hand under his stomach to prevent him from sitting. Stroke his chest with the fingers of your right hand. Praise him: "Good boy. Goood." Keep him standing for just a few seconds, then give him a treat.

5. Now guide him into a sit again.

Alternate the standing and sitting positions several times. Keep him in each position for only a few seconds. And you're done for that session!

As the days go by…

Gradually take your hands away (but be ready to grab him should he try to jump). If he breaks the sit or stand position when you remove your hands, just reposition him. Be patient but persistent.

If he gets really fussy and squirmy and resistant and won't settle, add a sharp "AH-ah" with a corrective technique, if necessary. But return to praise once he settles.

Touching your puppy all over his body

When your pup is reasonably proficient at holding the Sit and Stand positions, even if you still need to steady him a bit with one hand, you can add more *handling.*

With your puppy in a sitting position...

 Run your hand all over his body, and your fingers through his coat. Praise calmly ("Good") and give him a treat.

 Put one hand under his chin to lift his head up so you can peer into his eyes. Rub your index finger around the inner corner of his eyes, as though scraping off sleepy seeds. Praise calmly and give him a treat.

 Rub around the base of his ears. Peer inside his ears. Stroke the inside of his ears gently with your thumb. Praise calmly and give him a treat.

Still in a sitting position

Put one hand under his chin to steady his head. Say, "OPEN your mouth. OPEN." This doesn't mean he actually needs to open his mouth on command. It's just going to become a signal to him that you're going to be "poking around" in his mouth.

 Use the thumb of your other hand to lift up one side of his lip so you can peer at his teeth.

 Slide your fingers around his lips, getting him used to the odd sensation of his lips being pulled away from his teeth.

 Touch his teeth, gently rubbing them with the tip of your finger. Then praise calmly and give him a treat.

Say "Paw...Paw" and raise one of his front paws. Spread his toes and touch the webbing between them. Gently grasp each toenail between your thumb and index finger, just for a moment. Fold the paw gently backward so you can touch the *pad* of his foot.

 Repeat with his other front foot. Praise calmly and treat.

With your puppy in a standing position

 To handle his back feet, put your pup in his stand position. Say, "Paw...Paw" as you lift a rear foot and handle the toes, nails, and pads. Praise calmly and give him a treat.

> These handling exercises should be repeated on a regular basis until your puppy will sit still, or stand still, while you handle and touch any part of his body (including the testicles of a male pup). Your vet will love you for this!

If your pup tries to bite while being handled

If you've been diligently working your way through all of the chapters, your pup should not be trying to bite at this point. I recommend calling a local (balanced) trainer who can evaluate your pup personally and try to figure out what's going on.

Chapter 33

Let Go of Objects ("Give")

There will be times in your puppy's life when you want him to give up an object that he is clutching in his mouth.

"Jake, let go!" Kathy said in frustration. Her dog had pounced on her scarf and was clinging to it while Kathy tugged fruitlessly at the other end. *R-i-i-i-p-p!* went the scarf, and Kathy wailed in despair. With both hands, she tried to pry his jaws apart. Jake wagged his tail, but refused to let go.

How frustrating! Fortunately, there is a simple solution.

With your pup on leash, get him playing with a favorite toy. When he has it in his mouth, say in a cheerful voice, "Give" (or "Drop") and take hold of the toy with your hand.

Although he doesn't know what *Give* means yet, if he understands the proper leader-follower relationship he might automatically relinquish the toy out of respect. Say, "Yes!" or "Good!" and give him a treat if you happen to have one in your pocket. Then **give the toy back** and let him play some more before repeating.

Returning the toy after he has given it up makes a puppy more willing to give up things.

However, if he doesn't let go of the toy, if he clamps down or tries to engage in a tug of war with it...

...stand very still and hold your end of the toy as still as possible while repeating "Give" in a calm but firm voice.

Your stillness makes the game much less fun for your puppy—he sees that you're refusing to play, so he's more likely to let go. If he does, praise him just as cheerfully as if he had given up the toy in the first place. Then return it to him.

If holding the toy still didn't make him let go, and if he is not aggressive, work your way along the leash to his collar, which gives you control of his head. Say again, "Give" and open his mouth. There are two ways to get your pup to open his mouth:

 Pressure on his *lower* jaw. Place your hand under his jaw, palm up. Your thumb should be on one side of his jaw, your four fingers on the other side. Using all five fingers, press his LIPS inward against his TEETH as you say, "Give!" Most pups dislike the feeling of their lips pressing on their teeth and will open their mouth.

 Pressure on his *upper* jaw. Place your hand on TOP of his muzzle. Your thumb should be on one side of his muzzle, your four fingers on the other side, with the top of his muzzle nestled in the crook between your thumb and forefinger. Press all five fingers against his lips so that his lips press inward against his teeth. Again, his mouth should open.

If your pup has aggressive tendencies or you feel intimidated about fussing with his mouth, do something safer—hold up another toy and repeat "Give."

Many puppies are firm believers that the grass is always greener on the other side and will drop the object they have so they can have the new and "better" one. If he does that, praise him with enthusiasm and give him the second toy. Essentially you're trading with him.

> Now, this isn't ideal. You want your pup to drop an object *when told*, not just to get something else. But that should come as you continue to establish your leader-follower relationship.

Can you say "Out" instead of "Give"?

Sure. People who train dogs for protection work or competitive canine events often use "Out" to mean *let go*. It's a perfectly good word to use.

But most pet owners use "Out" to mean Go *outside in the yard* or Go *out to the bathroom*.

That's how I use it in this book. *Out* means outside, while *Give* means "let go of that object." But you can choose any word you want. For example, some owners use *Drop*.

I actually use both words. I say "*Give*" when my dog is close enough to me that I can reach out my hand to take the object.

I say "*Drop*" when my dog is farther away and I just want her to spit out whatever she has in her mouth. A dead bug, for example!

Chapter 34

Housebreaking Basics (Read this First)

If owners could choose only one skill they want their dog to have, *HOUSEBROKEN* would probably be first on the list.

The 2 major causes of housebreaking problems

- The #1 cause of housebreaking problems is **too much freedom** in the house.

- The #2 cause of housebreaking problems is an **improper routine.**

  Maybe you let your puppy loose in the yard to "go" on his own instead of *taking* him out.

  Maybe you don't take him out frequently enough. Every 1–2 hours is best.

  Maybe you wander around the yard or go for a walk, which distracts a pup from focusing on doing his business.

> Like anything else you're trying to teach your pup, housebreaking is a matter of creating a **good** routine for him, then sticking to it.

So let's start over. No matter how old your dog is, no matter how long the housebreaking issues have been going on, start implementing my housebreaking program right now as though your pup is new to your household.

Confinement and access—the two keys to housebreaking

 Confinement so your pup can't "go" in the WRONG place.

 Frequent access to the RIGHT place to "go."

1. **Confinement means that until your pup is 100% housebroken, he is *never* allowed to walk freely around the house.**

    He should be in a crate or pen or following you around the house on a leash. We talked about the why and how of this in Chapter 9, so be sure to reread that carefully.

    Confinement means every minute of every hour of every day—unless you're sitting with your puppy (on leash), playing with him (on leash), walking him (on leash), or otherwise interacting with him (on leash).

    Never allow a non-housebroken pup to be loose in the house. Not for one minute. Because if you take your eyes off him for one minute, he can pee on the rug or poop behind the recliner. Then you might not notice it for hours, so you can't correct him…and the bad habit is begun. The vast majority of housebreaking problems stem from freedom in the house.

2. **Frequent access to the RIGHT place to go** means you create a predictable routine of taking the puppy outside at least every 2 hours (every hour is even better). The more frequently you take him out, the quicker he will catch on.

   If you can't take your pup out every couple of hours, you need to provide an alternative *right place to go*—newspapers or a litter box in a wire pen or in a small room blocked by a gate or a doggy door (Chapter 36) so the pup can take *himself* out.

How long does it take to housebreak a puppy?

There is no one answer to that, just as there isn't a typical length of time for toilet-training a toddler. Some pups catch on in a matter of weeks, while others take many months.

Here are some factors that can affect how quickly a puppy is housebroken:

1. how diligent you are about confining him during the house-breaking period so he can't "go" in the wrong places

2. how frequently you take him to his potty area and praise/reward him when he eliminates there

3. how regular his feeding schedule is

4. his age

5. his size and breed

6. where you acquired him from

We already talked about (1) and (2), so let's briefly cover those other factors on the list.

Feeding schedule can affect housebreaking.

Don't leave food down for your puppy to nibble at throughout the day.

We talked about this in Chapter 20. "Free feeding" makes his digestive cycle unpredictable, which makes housebreaking more difficult.

Most puppies should eat three meals per day until 4 months old, then two meals per day thereafter.

Toy breed puppies (because they can have problems regulating their blood sugar) 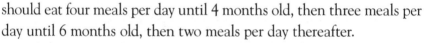 should eat four meals per day until 4 months old, then three meals per day until 6 months old, then two meals per day thereafter.

Adult dogs should eat twice a day, unless they have health problems that require three or four meals per day.

Feeding multiple meals doesn't mean you double or triple the amount of food he eats. You just take the total amount of food he should eat in a day and divide it into smaller portions.

> The last meal of the day should be no later than about 7:00 p.m. Give a last drink of water at the same time, then pick up the water. Then (hopefully) the puppy will be ready to pee at bedtime and not need to pee in the middle of the night. Hopefully!

Age can affect housebreaking.

Puppies under 3 months old can learn the *basic concept*, but they aren't yet *physically able* to do it. Puppies under 3 months old can't last longer than 2 to 3 hours during the day without eliminating. Their bladder and digestive system are not developed enough to "hold it" longer than that.

Nighttime is different. At night when a pup sleeps, his metabolism slows down and he can last longer without eliminating. Usually!

> So if you acquire an 8-week-old puppy, you're going to have a long wait before he can be considered house-broken. We're talking several *months.* That's one of the advantages of getting an older pup, who can better control his bladder and bowels.

On the other hand, if an older pup has been loose in the house and practicing bad habits for months, he might have better control of his organs…but swapping bad habits for good habits can take longer, compared to a young puppy with no bad habits.

Size can affect housebreaking.

Toy breeds are often difficult to housebreak. For example, Chihuahuas, Maltese, Yorkies, Shih Tzus, Maltipoos, Pomeranians, Pugs, MinPins, etc.

There are two reasons why toy dogs can be hard to housebreak:

- Many owners acquire them to "spoil" (always bad for a dog) and are reluctant to confine Little Snookums in a crate or pen, which can doom housebreaking right from the get-go.

  You see, when a toy dog is loose in the house, he finds it so easy to sneak behind a chair or under the coffee table, where it takes only a few seconds for the deed to be done. The result is hard to see and often goes undiscovered for days. By then the bad habit is firmly entrenched.

- The second reason tiny breeds can be hard to housebreak is their unnatural size. Humans have deliberately manipulated the genes of these breeds to shrink their structure, which affects the development and integrity of their internal organs, including their bladder and bowels.

So you should expect more problems with tiny dogs, especially if the pup is older and has been eliminating inappropriately in the house for some time.

> Be extra vigilant about confining toy dogs for however many months it takes. Some toys are not housebroken for many months, and some are never fully housebroken.

Your pup's breed can affect housebreaking

Besides toy breeds, a few other breeds tend to be slower to pick up the concepts of housebreaking.

I get a lot of desperate calls about Bichons, Havanese, Basset Hounds, Beagles, Boston Terriers, French Bulldogs, and Dachshunds.

Where you got your dog can affect housebreaking.

Dogs from puppy mills and pet shops can be hard to housebreak because they were raised in a small cage with no access to a separate potty area.

These unfortunate pups learned to eliminate wherever they happened to be standing, right there in their cage. Very bad habit.

A responsible breeder lays the foundations for proper housebreaking by offering their infant pups a separate area of newspapers or wood shavings.

These fortunate pups learned to toddle over and eliminate away from their sleeping blanket.

If you don't yet have your puppy, this caution might make you think twice about acquiring one from people who haven't laid the proper housebreaking foundation.

Chapter 35

Housebreaking (Outdoors)

> If you skipped ahead to this chapter, please go back
> and read Chapter 34: Housebreaking Basics. Important
> stuff there!

Teaching your puppy to go to the bathroom outside is best done using a crate plus frequent trips outdoors.

With this method, you take your pup outside, on leash, at least every couple of hours to a specific potty area, and you reward him when he eliminates there.

The more frequently you take him out, the faster he will learn.

The rest of the day and night, you confine him safely in a crate so he never has the chance to practice bad habits on the floors of your house. During the housebreaking period, he should be confined in his crate unless you're sitting with him, playing with him, walking him, or otherwise interacting with him.

He should never be loose in the house.

Sample housebreaking routine

The alarm wakes you at 6:00 a.m. Immediately you throw on clothes and head for your puppy's crate where he spent the night. But first, listen: is he quiet? You'll remember from the crate-training chapter that you should never let him out while he's barking.

If he's barking, you'll need to wait him out. Stay out of sight until he has been quiet for at least a couple of minutes. Then walk to his crate in a nonchalant manner. Once he sees you, he'll be excited. Don't speak to him or he might pee right away.

So say nothing other than a calm greeting: "Hi Jake." Open the crate door and say "Okay." As he starts through, quickly attach his leash, which you were smart enough to place on top of his crate when you put the pup to bed.

As you let your QUIET puppy out of the crate, don't pet him or play with him. Depending on how large/old he is, you might scoop him up and carry him, or you might let him walk. Either way, it's time for "You need to go OUT? Time to go OUT."

Immediately head for the door—always use the same door—to his potty area. First thing in the morning, get him out there as quickly as you can without running!

> Don't send a non-housebroken pup out in the yard to "go" on his own. This is one of the biggest mistakes owners make.

Unleashed dogs will run around and play instead of doing their business. And if they do "go" and you're not right there to praise and reward the puppy, you've missed a critical opportunity to reinforce the right behavior.

Always go to the same place in your yard.

Experiment to find out where your puppy eliminates best:

 Most pups prefer grass but they might dislike it in wet weather, or when the grass is too deep, or too short and prickly. Most puppies like to sniff around on grass, which is good because sniffing often leads to finding the right spot. But some pups get so preoccupied with sniffing that they don't focus on doing their business. For extremely sniffy, distractible pups, you might need a non-grass potty area.

 Many pups like dirt. Gravel might, or might not, be okay, depending on how comfortable it is to walk on.

 Many pups hate concrete, probably because it holds fewer interesting scents. But if you live in the city, concrete might be all that's available.

 Some pups want privacy. They feel exposed out in the open and prefer to go behind a bush or close beside a building.

 Some pups can't concentrate if there's activity going on nearby (for example, if there's a school across the street and the kids are out playing). Puppies who tend to gawk or bark need a quiet, boring spot.

 Some pups are too intimidated to eliminate if they can see another dog or hear one barking.

 Some dogs, especially toy breeds, dislike rain or snow—I usually make a covered potty area for these little guys.

> So find a spot where your puppy does well, then stick to that area. Having his own urine or stool scent in that place will remind him that this is where he eliminates.

Once there, say in a pleasant voice, "Find a spot" or "Go potty." Use a calm, pleasant voice, not stern or commanding. Your puppy needs to feel relaxed in order to be able to go!

Important...

 Don't let your puppy off the leash. This isn't a playtime routine. It's a potty break routine.

 Stand still. Root your feet in one place. Don't take your pup for a walk when you're housebreaking him. Go straight to the right spot, then stand still.

 Don't make eye contact with him or he will pay attention to you instead of concentrating on doing his business.

 Don't say anything to him, except to repeat your potty phrase several times. Other talking will only distract him.

Just stand there silently. Look off in the distance or count the clouds. Watch your puppy out of the corner of your eye. Hopefully, he will wander around you in a circle, sniffing the ground. If he sits or lies down or stands motionless, take a few steps in order to get him up and moving. Then stand still again.

If you walk around, he will look at these outings as a time for exploration and play rather than dedicated bathroom breaks. This is also why you use a 6-foot leash rather than a longer one. There are plenty of spots he can "go" within the length of a 6-foot leash.

How long should you stand there?

First thing in the morning, he should need to pee and poop...unless he has already gone in his crate overnight.

- Let's think positively. Let's say he kept his crate clean all night. What a good puppy! Now you know he needs to both pee and poop. So you should stay outside with him as long as it takes. Fortunately it usually doesn't take long.

- If he peed overnight in his crate, but didn't poop, he should be needing to do that now.

- Finally, if he both peed and pooped in his crate overnight... oh well. He may or may not "go" now. So keep an eye on the time. If after 10 minutes, he hasn't (at least) peed, bring him back inside and put him in his crate for 5 or 10 minutes. Then try him outside again. If you're persistent, he will learn that he must go to the bathroom—even a token drop or two—before he is allowed to run and play.

After a successful potty break

If and when he finally does go, praise him, "Good boy, go potty" AS he is going. You want to attach that phrase to the very act of eliminating.

Wait until he is completely finished, then reach into your pocket and pull out a treat. (If he sees the treat beforehand, or even if he sees your hand in your pocket, he might get distracted before he's done.) Give him the treat with lots of praise: "Yay! Good boy to go potty! Yay!"

If the weather is good, romp and play with him for a few minutes—his reward for a successful potty break.

If you're in a safely fenced yard **AND** if he *always* comes when you call him (Chapter 18), you can let him off leash to romp and play.

Otherwise leave the leash on, although you might swap it out for a 15- or 20-foot leash to give him more room.

After a successful potty break and activity session, give your pup a drink of water and put him in his crate (Chapter 13) or pen (Chapter 14). Or he can stay connected to you via the leash (Chapter 9).

For the last potty break of the day, I aim for 11 pm.

IMPORTANT: Keep a written log of every potty break and its result, including the time. Something simple like: Tue, Jun 6, 6:00 a.m., 1, 2 (where 1 is urination and 2 is defecation).

Chapter 36

Housebreaking (Doggy Door)

If you skipped ahead to this chapter, please go back and read Chapter 34: Housebreaking Basics. Important stuff there!

Caution: Unless you live way out in the country away from neighbors, don't give your puppy access to a doggy door if he's a barker. Some owners who work all day install a doggy door, then congratulate themselves for providing their pup with a bathroom. Except that he goes outside and barks all day! Then your neighbors complain to the police, animal control, or your homeowners association. I certainly would.

Ideal set-up for a doggy door

In my house, we have a mudroom off the kitchen. In the mudroom is a doggy door leading outside to a small, fenced "potty yard."

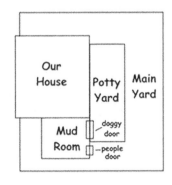

Why is the potty yard *small* and *separated from the main yard?* Because if a pup can go through the doggy door into a big yard, he will want to run and explore rather than focus on "pottying."

It's also unsafe to leave a puppy loose in a large yard with no one there to supervise him. This is how so many pups escape, or get stolen, or swallow something they shouldn't.

But as long as you're home to supervise, having a doggy door can be very convenient.

After we housebreak our dogs using the crate method (Chapter 35), we teach them to use a doggy door to take themselves outside to potty.

> Notice that we teach them how to use the doggy door
> *after* they are housebroken.

You can also teach a *NON*-housebroken puppy how to use a doggy door. But it's much easier to teach the door *after* he has already learned that **outdoors** is the place to go to the bathroom.

I'll show you how to do it both ways.

First, the easiest way…

Teaching an already housebroken pup to use a doggy door

First, remove the heavy flap on the door (or tie the flap up out of the way) so your puppy has free access through the hole into his potty yard. The flap can be put back later, after your pup has learned how this hole-in-the-wall works.

If he is reluctant to go through the hole at first, you can stand inside the house with him while your spouse stands outside in the potty yard, crouched near the open hole. The two of you then take turns waving treats through the hole and calling him so that he runs through it successfully and gets rewarded each time.

Once he has the hang of the open hole, you may want to hang a light towel or cloth over the opening for a few more days, as a gradual transition toward the heavier vinyl flap. Use treats to teach him that he can push through the cloth and that he only has to poke his nose through it or under it in order to scramble through.

Eventually you'll move on to the heavier flap. Though it looks daunting at first, rest assured that even toy dogs (like my Chihuahua) can move it.

Periodically throughout the day, at times when you would normally take your dog out for a potty break, ask him, "Do you need to go OUT? Go OUT. Go OUT."

Walk toward the doggy door, using hand motions to encourage him to go through. If necessary, lead him through the door by the collar.

To speed up the learning curve, *you should go outside too.* Pick a spot outside to stand where you can observe your puppy, but don't interact with him. Let him go about his business, which hopefully will include going to the bathroom.

The reason you're out there is to *reward him* when he goes to the bathroom outside. Make a big deal out it: "Yay! Good boy!" Give him a treat. Then romp and play with him or take him for an enjoyable walk. In this way, he learns that he must go to the bathroom—even a token drop or two—before playtime.

> Do you see the advantage of having the small potty yard inside the main yard? It helps your pup focus on eliminating rather than running around playing. By the way, you can also install a cover or roof over the potty yard, which keeps rain and snow out. For some hard-to-housebreak breeds, a covered potty yard can be a must.

Teaching a NON-housebroken pup to use a doggy door

In the previous section, I explained how to coax a housebroken puppy to use the doggy door. That section assumed a pup who already understood the concept of housebreaking (i.e., that he's supposed to go to the bathroom *outdoors).*

It's trickier to teach both housebreaking and the doggy door at the same time. It is do-able for most pups, but it can take longer and more problems may crop up in the process.

First, wrap an exercise pen (ex-pen) around the doggy door such that your puppy can be confined to the pen with constant access to the small potty yard via the doggy door. During the day, this is where he should stay whenever you're not directly interacting with him. See Chapter 14 for more info on ex-pens.

To teach your puppy to go through the doggy door, follow the directions in the previous section of this chapter.

At night, your pup should sleep in his crate. You do NOT want him outdoors at night. He can get into all kinds of trouble—he can get loose, bark, get bitten by a rabid raccoon, etc. All family dogs belong indoors at night.

In fact, I recommend securely *closing* the doggy door at night. These doors come with a metal panel that slides down over the hole (on the inside) and blocks it from nighttime critters like cats, coons, and skunks.

Chapter 37

Housebreaking (Indoors)

> If you skipped ahead to this chapter, please go back and read Chapter 34: Housebreaking Basics. Important stuff there!

Caution: Encouraging a dog to pee and poop on newspapers or in a litter box is teaching him to pee and poop *inside your house.*

If you're planning to let him do this throughout his life, that's fine. But some owners only want their dog to "go" indoors when he's very young. Then they want to transition him into going outdoors.

Yes, many dogs can make that transition, but some dogs get very confused. So be aware that it might not be as easy as you think to first tell your pup he *can* "go" in the house, then later tell him he can't. Put yourself in your dog's place and you can see the potential for confusion.

When you don't have a choice:

Sometimes your hand is forced. Maybe you work all day. Or maybe you

live in a high-rise condo or your weather is rotten much of the time
and you can't take your puppy outside every couple of hours all through
the day and evening.

In such cases, you need to provide your pup with **constant** access
to a bathroom spot.

 This might be a small potty yard outdoors which your pup
can access through a doggy door (Chapter 36).

 **Or it can be an indoor bathroom. This chapter is about
providing an indoor bathroom for your (smallish) dog.**

Indoor bathroom options

Let's start with a quick list. I'll explain more about each option in
a minute. An indoor bathroom can be...

- a small fenced area *indoors,* filled with pine mulch or turf,
  where a small dog can walk around a bit as though he were
  truly outdoors. If you have a good space for this, it's the most
  natural option for a dog.

- a plastic litter box. For tiny dogs, this could be a plastic storage
  bin from a discount store, whereas slightly larger (but still
  smallish) dogs might need a plastic kiddie pool. The litterbox
  can be filled with real or artificial turf, or with pine mulch or
  cat litter. There are even companies that sell fancy litter boxes.

- "pee pads" or weewee pads, which are soft pads impregnated
  with an odor that encourages dogs to pee on them.

- newspapers spread on the floor.

Let's talk about each of those options.

Indoor potty yard

Here is an example of a homemade potty yard in a mud room. A heavy tarp was placed atop the vinyl floor, and a couple of inches of pine mulch was laid on top of the tarp. The yard is scooped every day and the mulch completely changed every month.

The sides of the yard are high, because some dogs will back up to the wall of a confined area and leave their deposits against, or over, the wall.

I should also mention that indoor bathrooms work better for female dogs, since males who lift their leg can spray urine everywhere. With leg-lifting males, the yard definitely needs high sides. Some owners include a vertical "pee pole" (covered with plastic) in the center of the yard.

Indoor litter box

Now I'll admit that an indoor potty yard is not the loveliest thing to look at! A regular litter box, like a cat's box, looks more appealing.

Unfortunately, many dogs don't like to "go" in such a small area. If you've ever watched a dog hunting for the right bathroom spot, you know how they like to wander around in circles and sniff!

So litter boxes work best for tiny dogs such as Chihuahuas, Maltese, and Yorkies. Even then, the bigger the box, the better. As with potty yards, the sides of the box should be quite high, or else you may find stools eliminated over the edge and onto your floor. A regular cat box is too shallow for dogs.

I recommend making your own box from a deep plastic storage bin. Cut a squared-off U-shape in one side to make a step-over entrance, leaving enough of the box below the entrance to hold the litter in the box.

In the picture, you can see a plastic storage bin being used as a litter box. Actually, it's TWO storage bins, one stacked on top of the other. The lower bin is intact, while the upper bin had its bottom cut out of it, then its four walls were hot-glued onto the lower box to make the whole unit taller.

Warning: Don't use clumping kitty litter!

Clumping litter hardens into a compact little ball when it gets wet, (i.e., when urine soaks into it). Clumping litter is easy to scoop up and much less wasteful of litter, compared to the old traditional clay litter.

Unfortunately, we now know that when a dog or cat licks clumping litter off its paws or coat and swallows it, the litter gets wet (from saliva and stomach fluid). Then it can **clump** in his stomach.

You can find out more about the dangers of clumping kitty litter by doing a Google search.

So what kind of litter should you use? I recommend litter made from recycled newspaper.

A good brand is *Yesterday's News Unscented.* It's nontoxic, dust-free, super-absorbent, and environmentally friendly. It's very popular; you can find it at any pet store and also at health food stores.

Commercial litter boxes

Some companies market litter box "systems" where you get the box for a one-time charge, and then the company periodically ships you replacement "turf" to lay inside the box. The turf might be natural, or artificial like indoor/outdoor carpeting.

The photos show a flat surface that resembles a miniature golf putting green, with no sides or walls to speak of. So unless your dog happens to go right in the middle, I would expect an awful lot of "misses" and a messy floor around the box. But I can't speak from experience, so...

Pee Pads

Also called **wee wee pads** or housetraining pads, these swatches of cloth come pretreated with an odor that resembles urine, which (sort of) encourages pups to pee on them.

I dislike these pads immensely.

- I dislike them because they're tossed on the floor, then the puppy is allowed to wander loose in a big room (or the entire house) and is expected to find the pad whenever he needs to "go." This just sets him up for failure.

- I dislike them because they're too small. Dogs like to sniff and circle around to find just the right spot. It's unrealistic to expect a pup to find the center of a small cloth and eliminate such that the entire deposit hits that small space.

- And I dislike them because they encourage a dog to pee or poop on soft things…like carpets, sofa cushions, and the blanket on your bed.

> When I'm called upon to solve housebreaking issues, I often find that these cloth pads are in use, or have been in use. In my experience, they *cause* more problems than they solve.

Newspapers spread on the floor

In this old traditional method of housebreaking, you lay down newspapers on the floor. The problem is that owners often want their pup to go on newspapers when he's young, then start going outdoors when he gets older.

This works okay for some dogs, but confuses others. So before you start laying down newspapers, be sure you're prepared to deal with potential housebreaking confusion in the future. You shouldn't punish a confused dog. Instead, you should start from the very beginning with the crate-training or doggy-door method.

How to teach your pup to use an indoor bathroom

You'll want to give him *constant* access to his bathroom. The best way to do that is to wrap an exercise pen (Chapter 14) snugly around his litterbox, little potty yard, or newspapers.

Until he is fully housebroken, your puppy should stay in the pen all the time—unless you're sitting with him, playing with him, walking him, grooming him, or otherwise fully interacting with him. This ensures that he never has the chance to learn or practice bad habits on the floors of your house.

An alternative is to confine the pup to a small laundry or mudroom that's blocked with a baby gate.

A room works okay with newspapers because they're spread everywhere so the pup can't "miss" going on them. A room works less well with a litter box because with more free space, the puppy can easily go on the floor *outside* the box.

How to teach your pup to use a litter box enclosed in a pen

1. Shape the exercise pen tightly around the litter box so the box fills the entire pen except for a small blanket or bed, a water bowl, and a toy. Leave no open space. Most pups don't want to soil their blanket, so they will almost always go in the box if you give them no other choice.

2. Place your puppy in the pen. If he barks, see Chapter 13. If he jumps on the sides of the pen, see Chapter 14.

3. Once he's calm and quiet, occasionally encourage him to step into the litter box by holding a treat in front of his nose and leading him in. Once he's in, praise and give him the treat. It's okay if he steps right back out. You simply want him to get used to stepping in the box and associating it with good things.

4. Whenever you see him step into the box on his own, even to play, praise him. "Yes. Good boy." But don't get him all revved up! If you see him go to the bathroom, that's the time to praise with enthusiasm and give a treat!

5. After he has been using the box reliably for a week or so, expand the size of the pen *just a little* so he has a little more room to play. If he makes a mistake by eliminating on the newly-open floor inside the pen, shrink the pen again and give him another few days of practice before you try expanding again. Don't rush it!

> Remember, while you're housebreaking him, he should be outside the pen only when you're interacting with him. He should not be walking freely around the house.

Chapter 38

Housebreaking (Cleaning Up Accidents)

Suppose your puppy goes to the bathroom in his crate, in his pen, or on the floor of your house.

Cleaning with soap and water does not get rid of the **microscopic odor particles** that will attract your pup back to the soiled area.

White vinegar mixed with water does a decent job, but the best type of cleaner is an *enzymatic cleaner* that uses enzymes to break down and "eat" the odor particles.

My favorite enzymatic cleaner is *Nature's Miracle*, which you can find at any pet supply store. It comes in a convenient spray bottle. Use paper towels to blot up the urine or pick up the stool, then spray on the Nature's Miracle. Leave it to do its work for 30 minutes before patting the spot dry with another paper towel.

> Don't use a household cleaner with ammonia in it. Urine itself contains ammonia, so your puppy is *attracted* to ammonia products. That's the opposite of what you want!

If you SEE your puppy peeing or pooping in the wrong place, clap your hands and say, "AH-ah!" Loud claps, loud voice! He might be startled enough to actually stop peeing or pooping (though that doesn't happen often). But if he does stop, quickly scoop him up and carry him to the proper potty area.

If your loud clap and loud voice doesn't stop him, oh well!

- If you're just starting housebreaking with him, there's nothing you can do now but clean up the mess and review your housebreaking schedule to see what went wrong.

- If your pup is at least 4 months old, and if you've been working on housebreaking for a while now, and if you're sure the pup understands what *No* means, you can **very quickly** scoot him around to see the misdeed while you say, "No." As long as your pup really does understand what *No* means, a mild reprimand can be effective.

- **But don't yell. Don't hit the puppy. And absolutely, positively, don't rub his nose in it!**

Always remember that ***prevention*** of housebreaking accidents is far more effective than trying to correct after the fact. **Every accident in the house is a step backward in housebreaking.** Follow my housebreaking program carefully and don't let a non-housebroken dog walk around loose indoors.

Chapter 39

Housebreaking Problems

Problem: your puppy is reluctant to eliminate outdoors.

Is your pup eliminating mostly indoors in his crate? Is he reluctant to pee or poop outdoors? If so, we need to focus on getting him to "go" outdoors. That should cut down on his eliminating indoors.

- Increase your frequency of trips outside. Say, every hour instead of every two hours. If he doesn't go when you take him out, put him in his crate for 10 or 15 minutes, then try again. And again.

- Some puppies are very fussy about their footing. They might dislike walking on short mown grass, which can be prickly on tender feet. Or they might dislike walking in longer grass. To a toy breed, walking through long grass feels like walking through a wild jungle.

- Some pups are nervous about eliminating when they can see or hear other dogs.

- Some pups detest rain or snow, and might need a covered bathroom spot. Many toy breeds hate cold/wet weather so much that you should either construct a roof or teach them to use an indoor litter box (Chapter 37).

- Leave (or place) one of your dog's stools in the area you want him to go. If he sniffs at it, praise him quietly. "Good boy, go potty."

- Make sure you're not walking around. Stand still and let your pup wander around you in a circle within the length of the 6-foot leash.

- Make sure you're not letting the pup just stand there doing nothing. Take a few steps in any direction and use the leash to gently get your dog moving. A puppy can't go to the bathroom when he's just standing or sitting still.

- Make sure you're not talking to your puppy, looking into his eyes, or touching him. Don't be a distraction.

- Make sure you're praising and rewarding with a treat immediately when your puppy has either peed or pooped. But don't fish around in your pocket while he's still "going" or you might distract him. Wait until he's done before you even reach for the treat.

Problem: your puppy is perfectly willing to eliminate outdoors, but also goes in his crate.

Look on the bright side: at least he's doing half of it right! Now we just need to get him to STOP going indoors.

- Make sure the crate is small enough. Your puppy should have just enough room to turn around and lie down comfortably, but no extra room.

- Make sure you're taking him out frequently enough—at least every two hours. Every hour if you can manage it.

- Make sure there is no food or water in the crate.

- Make sure there's no bedding in the crate. It absorbs urine, which then allows your pup to sleep in greater comfort after he pees. You would rather he be a little uncomfortable—it's an incentive to keep his crate clean.

- Monitor his mealtime/potty schedule. For example, maybe you're waiting a little too long after he eats. Every puppy is different in how soon he needs to eliminate after eating.

Problem: your pup is peeing in his crate multiple times a day

If you're taking your puppy out frequently, but he's still peeing both indoors and out, have your vet test for a urinary tract infection and bladder stones.

If you've ever had a UTI, you know how awful it feels to have those sudden, uncontrollable urges. You might produce hardly any urine, yet 5 minutes later you feel that urge again.

When your pup's housebreaking issues are mostly urination issues, get his urinary system checked out ASAP.

Problem: your puppy is doing good with housebreaking during the day, but still eliminates in his crate overnight.

 Pick up water at 7:00 p.m. Experiment with meal times. You might try his evening meal at 6:00 or 7:00 p.m., then out to potty every two hours until midnight. Hopefully he will move his bowels during one of those outings. Conversely, you might push his evening meal up to 10:00 p.m., then out to potty at midnight and hope he will sleep all night without needing to poop. There is no one "right" schedule that fits all dogs.

 Make sure you get your puppy outside *first thing in the morning,* like at 6:00 a.m. Wear your clothes to bed, if necessary, so you can get him out fast. Two minutes can make all the difference in the earliest stages of housebreaking.

Problem: your puppy is pooping more than three times a day.

He shouldn't be. Puppies might poop too much when they have a digestive ailment that needs checking out. But it's much more likely that they're simply being fed more food than their body needs, so the excess is coming out.

Pups also poop more when their food contains ingredients that they don't digest well, such as wheat, corn, rice, or soybeans. Grains and cereals often go right through a dog, producing a lot of waste. See the feeding chapter in my book, *11 Things You Must Do Right To Keep Your Dog Healthy and Happy.*

> Overfeeding or feeding the wrong food can definitely interfere with housebreaking, so it's important to correct those issues.

Are there some dogs who simply can't be housebroken?

Yes, some so-called "dirty dogs" regularly eliminate in their crate, then sit or lie in it without seeming to notice or care.

You can do everything right and these dogs seem to have no clue that they're supposed to keep their sleeping quarters clean.

Most often, a "dirty dog" is one whose early upbringing failed to lay the foundations for proper housebreaking.

The dog might have come from a pet shop, a puppy mill, or a breeder who didn't offer a separate area of newspapers or wood shavings, where the infant pups could toddle over and eliminate away from their sleeping blanket.

If you don't yet have your puppy, this warning might make you think twice about acquiring one from dubious sources.

> But many owners are certain they have one of these hopeless dogs when in fact it's the *owner* who isn't doing something right. A frustrated owner will swear he's tried everything. But when I arrive for a consultation, I almost always find one (or more) things the owner is doing that should be altered.

It's actually good news how quickly most pups will respond if you just do that one little thing you skipped over. So don't give up hope until you really have tried *everything* in these housebreaking chapters.

Chapter 40

Housebreaking (More Freedom in the House)

Owners are often eager for housebreaking to be over so their pup "can have more freedom" in the house. But why? What do they imagine their loose pup is going to be doing that's so wonderful?

When I visit friends whose pups are loose in the house, I very seldom see a calm, secure, well-behaved dog.

Instead I see pups with excited, aroused mental states, looking out the window for things to bark at, demanding to be let outside or inside, begging for food, shoving their head into someone's lap demanding petting, or scouting through different rooms looking for things to chew or hidden places to pee.

So even if your pup is completely housebroken by 6 or 7 months old, he should not be loose in the house (Chapter 9).

If you grant freedom too soon, a sudden string of accidents or unwanted behavior can set back his future behavior in a hurry.

But if your puppy is at least 10 months old AND has not had an accident in his crate or in the house for at least a month...

...when you're reading a book or working on your computer

...when he has just recently peed outside and isn't due to poop

...when he normally would be in his crate or practicing *Place*

...let him loose in the room with you.

But take precautions!

 Close the door so he can't wander elsewhere.

 While you're working, look up frequently to see how he's doing. If he suddenly starts sniffing the floor or begins  walking in circles, take him out to his potty area right away. You need to learn your particular pup's signs that he needs to go out.

 After an hour or so, take him outside. If he at least pees, praise him lavishly and give him another period of freedom in the same room. However, if he doesn't go, put him in his crate or pen for awhile, then try him outside again. Once he has successfully gone outside, give him another period of freedom in the room with you.

> As you can see, you don't throw your house open to him all at once. One room at a time. One hour at a time. And if he has an accident when you're giving him more freedom, he's not ready! Go back to crating or leashing for a while.

Chapter 41

Urinating When Excited or Nervous

The good news is that this behavior is NOT a housebreaking problem. **The bad news** is that your pup has no control over it.

Excitable urination

An excited dog, especially a young one, doesn't always have complete control of his bladder. If he's very happy to see someone, his bladder may accidentally let go when the person reaches toward him.

Submissive urination

This is an *instinct* in the canine species. A submissive canine, upon meeting a more dominant one, often crouches and releases a little urine, which is a canine *social signal* that says to the dominant dog, "Don't hurt me! I accept your superiority."

A submissive dog may do the same thing when a *person* bends over him, or reaches toward him, or raises their voice at him. Submissive urination is most common in young and adolescent dogs, and in gentle, soft-tempered dogs.

How to deal with excitable or submissive urination

A piddling pup is NOT doing this on purpose! It is an instinctive behavior that he has no control over. If you punish him, it only makes him *more* submissive and *more* prone to piddling.

When you have a pup with this behavior, you need to be casual and calm around him.

Keep your voice calm and matter-of-fact. Don't get him excited!

When you greet him, **don't make eye contact.** Look over his head or past him, rather than directly at him.

Don't reach your hand toward his head or body.

Keep his leash on—he can drag it around the house as long as you're monitoring him. This allows you to control him without needing to put your hands on his body.

Build the pup's confidence by teaching him how to conquer obstacles and play challenging games such as *Tug* (both are covered in my book, *Teach Your Dog 100 English Words*).

> Submissive urination and excitable urination are most common in puppies and adolescents. If you don't punish the youngster for it, it usually goes away with maturity.

Unfortunately, "usually" doesn't mean "always." Sometimes this behavior persists even when the dog is an adult. Then all you can do is continue managing it as best as you can.

Just remember that punishing it never helps, but only makes things worse.

Chapter 42
Marking (Leg-Lifting Against Objects)

Puppies don't start lifting their leg to urinate until adolescence, which begins around 6 or 7 months old in smaller breeds, and around 10 to 12 months old in larger breeds.

A dog lifts his leg in order to spray his urine as high as possible, thereby "marking" his territory. He's saying, "Hey, all you sniffers, I was here! I'm One Big Bad Dude and I claim this territory."

Some dogs become *compulsive* markers. They might haul you toward every tree and fire hydrant to leave their scent here…and here…and here. This is very disrespectful to you, the "leader."

Compulsive marking can morph into displays of dominance or aggression toward other dogs.

Compulsive markers might also mark *inside your house,* especially if you have multiple dogs in the home and you're allowing them to decide "which one's the boss." (Chapter 46)

Certain breeds (such as terriers and toys) are more prone to compulsive marking. Some tiny dogs dash around like little wind-up toys, lifting their leg busily on every vertical blade of grass, or even against people's ankles!

As far as gender, compulsive marking is most common in non-neutered males, but many neutered males do it, too.

Even females (whether spayed or not) are known to mark, but because of their anatomy, they just kind of lift one hind foot and dribble. Their urine doesn't go any higher, but they seem satisfied that it has.

What to do about excessive marking:

Marking territory is essentially an instinctive behavior. The dog does it without thinking.

That might sound like there's nothing you can do about it.

But dogs do many instinctive behaviors that we must say *No* to. *No* growling over a bone. *No* digging holes in the yard. *No* jumping the fence to chase a female dog in heat. *No* killing the neighbor's sheep. Those are all instinctive behaviors, but we can stop all of them with corrective techniques.

By holding the dog accountable for ALL of his behaviors, we help him to **pay attention** to what he does, to **be aware** of what he does— which means his behaviors become conscious choices rather than mindless instincts.

> Once a behavior is a conscious choice, the dog can choose to do it. Or not. He will make that choice based on consequences.

Does anything good happen when he pees against the kitchen table? Yes, he feels satisfied that he's left his scent there.

Does anything bad happen? That's up to you. Move toward your dog assertively and correct with a sharp, "AH-ah! No!" and a firm jerk on the leash or one of the other corrective techniques (Chapter 5) that work for your particular dog.

If you provide the right negative consequence—one that outweighs the reward he receives from peeing against the table—most dogs will decide that marking isn't worth it.

At least when it comes to marking the *table.* Dogs aren't always adept about generalizing. You might need to methodically correct marking the sofa, marking the door frame, marking the wheels of your car, etc.

This far into the book, you probably know that a dog who is marking **indoors** should not be loose in the house. He should be in a crate or pen (Chapter 13), or practicing his impulse control on *Place* (Chapter 16), or leashed to you so that he must follow you around (Chapter 9).

> Indoor markers, like all misbehaving dogs, need tons of structure, routines, and consequences in their lives. Establishing the proper leader-follower relationship is essential.

Work through everything on the *Cheat Sheet* list in Chapter 4. The dog should not be allowed on your bed or furniture (Chapter 21). He should not be allowed to demand petting (Chapter 22). He should "Wait" for your permission before going through doors and gates (Chapter 15). He must be polite at meal time (Chapter 20).

Clean marked areas with an enzymatic cleaner such as *Nature's Miracle.* Soap and detergents don't remove the microscopic odor particles that can attract your dog back to the same area.

If your dog only marks outdoors, that's easier to control. Take him for **structured** walks only (Chapter 12) where he isn't allowed to eliminate during the *walking* part of the excursion.

Neutering?

Neutering doesn't solve compulsive marking in most dogs. Negative consequences and the proper leader-follower relationship solves compulsive marking.

Now, in toy breeds (Chihuahua, Yorkie, etc.), neutering can *sometimes* help with compulsive marking.

However, there are health risks associated with neutering. In particular, if you neuter too early, it predisposes dogs to serious health risks later in life. For some eye-opening information on neutering, check out my canine health book, *11 Things You Must Do Right To Keep Your Dog Healthy and Happy.*

Belly bands

Sometimes I get a desperate call from someone who has been living with a compulsive marker for many years. Typically this is an elderly owner with a small older dog who has a long-standing habit of lifting his leg in the house (along with many other issues).

We go over all the leadership things on the *Cheat Sheet* (Chapter 4) and the owner promises to do her best.

But with severe arthritis, she has a hard time getting around and when I check back with her, she admits that she hasn't been able to follow the program. She asks if there's anything I can suggest to just protect her furniture.

So I tell her about **belly bands.** These are pieces of absorbent cloth that you wrap around a male dog's private parts when he's indoors. If he lifts his leg, he'll soak the band, but not your furniture. You can buy them online—search for "original belly bands for dogs."

Belly bands might be the only solution if an owner can't (or won't) follow the program of structure, consequences, and leadership that would truly solve the problem.

Chapter 43

Socializing Your Pup to Get Along with the World

You've probably been told that you need to take your puppy out of the house and socialize him with other people, other dogs, and other environments.

That's true. But the word *socialize* can mean different things.

The traditional meaning of socialization

Some owners define *socialization* as making their puppy more **social,** more **friendly** toward people they encounter on their walks.

To accomplish this, you might sit on a bench at the park or at a shopping center, and when someone passes by, you encourage the person to pet your puppy and to give him a treat.

Important! If you have a small dog, ask the person to turn their hand so their palm is facing UP and then to rub their fingers against the dog's **throat and chest,** rather than patting his head. Demonstrate with your own hand.

Small dogs (quite understandably) hate giant hands descending from the sky onto their tiny heads. If people try to *pat* them on the head, they may become both hand-shy and head-shy.

So that's the traditional method of socialization. But what might happen if you teach your puppy that strangers are a source of positive attention and treats?

Well, if your pup is an outgoing extrovert, he might begin scanning for people during every walk. He might get excited when he sees someone, eagerly whining and pulling on the leash. Which means he is less focused on YOU. And all those words you've taught him, the ones he obeys so well in your house and yard? When he gets distracted by other people, he probably pays less attention to your words.

I have a dog like that. She was very outgoing as a puppy, so I chose to socialize her in the traditional way, by encouraging her to go to strangers and be friendly. And sure enough, when she's greeting other people, she pays a lot less attention to me.

But that's okay with me because she's a small gentle dog, easy to manage even when she does get distracted. And I love that she has this knack for making other people smile when she greets them as her long-lost friends.

Also, I have a trick up my sleeve when I want her to stop paying attention to other people. I begin a **structured walk** (Chapter 12) where she must pay attention to me only. She has learned that when I announce a structured walk, meet-and-greet time is over and she needs to focus on me again.

A different meaning of socialization

But I also have dogs who are more introverted, reserved, and stand-offish. These dogs don't want to greet a stranger as a long-lost friend. In fact, they would prefer that strangers just leave them alone. Introverted dogs should not be forced to **interact** with people they don't even know.

So if you prefer, here's a different kind of socialization

You still take your puppy to different environments, different social settings, such as the park, or downtown, or a shopping center.

 But you don't allow him to *interact* with anyone, and you don't allow anyone to interact with your pup.

Instead, you work on all the words the pup knows ("Heel. Sit. Come.") and you use treats plus leash guidance to make sure he pays attention to you and ignores everyone else.

With this type of socialization, your goal is NOT to make your pup "friendly." Your goal is to teach him to *behave* (to pay attention, no barking, jumping, lunging) in different social settings:

 a busy sidewalk with pedestrians

 a shopping mall

 a suburban neighborhood with kids riding bicycles and dogs barking behind fences

 a park where children are kicking a soccer ball while their parents hoot and applaud on the sidelines

In these social settings, you want your pup to focus on *you* and to simply "share space" with everyone else. You want him to view everything else as harmless, meaningless background noise. Because *you* are the only one he interacts with, that means *you* are the only one who gives him treats—never a stranger.

> This kind of socialization is practiced by many trainers of world-class competition dogs, police dogs, and dogs for the disabled.

These trainers take their pup everywhere, but they don't allow anyone to invade his space or try to pet him. If a stranger approaches, the trainer whips out a tasty treat and gets the dog focused on the trainer rather than the stranger. The pup learns that when he sees strangers, his *owner* will give him treats. Seeing a stranger then becomes a GOOD thing to the pup...but not someone to interact with.

And if a stranger tries to pet the dog anyway? The trainer says, "Ma'am, he's in training right now, so I'd appreciate it if you don't pet him. That would be helpful to us, thank you."

Risks of socializing with strangers

We've already talked about two risks of letting your puppy interact with strangers:

1. You're encouraging the puppy to pay attention to other people instead of to you.

2. An introverted pup may feel trapped if you let lots of strangers pet him.

There's also a third risk.

3. A stranger might do something the puppy finds startling or scary, which can mess up the pup's temperament.

Sometimes all it takes is one negative experience for a very sensitive or
impressionable pup to be wary of all
strangers, or strangers who resemble the
one who startled him.

The puppy starts tucking his tail and
avoiding people, or threatening them with
blustery barks to make them go away.

> Owners often leap to the conclusion that their shy or
> aggressive rescue dog must have been abused. But it's far
> more common that he was simply startled or handled
> inappropriately at an impressionable age.

What might a stranger do that could negatively affect your puppy?
He might rush in and invade the pup's space. He might try to hug or
kiss the pup. He might try to pick the pup up. He might pat the pup
(thump-thump!) on the head. He might wave his arms or break into
a loud, rollicking laugh. He might make woofing sounds at the pup.
People do all sorts of daft things around dogs.

How do you avoid things like that happening?

- Well, you can try to manage every interaction carefully.
  "Excuse me, I'm getting my puppy used to people. Would you
  be willing to hand him this treat? But please don't touch him
  yet because he's still a little nervous around people."

  The problem is that many people can't or won't follow
  instructions.

- Or you might decide to take your puppy only to places where
  you know the people well and can trust them to carefully
  follow your instructions. Assuming you know such people!

- Or you might decide that you won't allow any stranger to interact with your pup when you're walking him in public.

Now, that doesn't mean your puppy becomes a hermit. In your own home and yard, your friends and relatives who visit can certainly pet and play with your pup, if he enjoys that.

Now, even if he's more reserved, he still must learn to accept handling when you say so. Else how could a veterinarian or groomer or boarding kennel worker take care of him? You've taught him to *Sit* and *Stand* while you examine his ears, mouth, paws, etc. (Chapter 32). You should occasionally ask a responsible friend to do the same thing while you direct and guide the pup into the right positions.

> As responsible guardians, we must teach our dogs how to be calm and accepting in the real world that we all live in.

Be a good role model for your dog.

Whether you decide to let your pup interact with strangers or not, **you** should still interact with strangers.

Smile and say "Hello" to passersby. Ask them what time it is. Comment on the weather.

Why? Because you want your puppy to see that you're happy to see people.

If you, the leader, are relaxed and confident, your pup, the follower, will conclude that the world is nothing to worry about. If you're tense and anxious, he is more likely to be, too.

Loosen your puppy's leash.

One of the most common mistakes owners make is holding their puppy on a tight leash around other people or other dogs.

- **A taut leash can make dogs *more* aggressive.** When your pup can feel your presence (literally) through the leash, he feels bolder about threatening someone else because you're there to "back him up." The tight leash is his umbilical cord.

- **A taut leash can make anxious dogs *more* anxious.** The pup feels trapped, which makes him more fearful.

- Finally, a taut leash communicates to your puppy that *you're* concerned about the situation—which makes **him** concerned about the situation.

> So don't hold your pup tightly beside you. Use the leash techniques you learned in Chapter 11 to keep the leash loose.

Correct inappropriate behavior.

The most important message to convey to your puppy is this:

"You don't need to **like** people or other dogs. But you must *accept* them. You cannot express your negative feelings through inappropriate **behavior**."

Really, it's that simple.

If your pup dislikes strangers, **having** those feelings is fine. But he needs to keep them to himself.

He may not:

- growl, bark, or woof suspiciously

- lunge toward anyone

- bolt fearfully to the end of the leash, trying to escape

- stand up on his hind legs, pawing at you to be picked up

A puppy who is doing any of those things is not practicing calmness and is not trusting **you**, the leader, to handle the situation. That's a no-no, so use whichever corrective techniques work for your particular pup to get him standing quietly beside you on a loose leash.

If you can't control the puppy with a regular buckle collar, switch to one of the alternatives I recommended in Chapter 11.

Don't, don't don't...

Don't reassure a puppy who is displaying inappropriate behavior. This is a huge mistake that owners make.

> Don't say soothing things like "It's okay, I'm here, nobody's going to hurt you." It might seem like a perfectly natural thing to do, but it isn't. It makes things worse.

A soothing voice and petting are interpreted by a dog as **positive reinforcement** of whatever behavior he's exhibiting. Dogs repeat behaviors that bring them rewards. If you reward nervous or aggressive behavior with soothing or petting or treats, you're going to see **more** nervous or aggressive behavior.

In a stressful situation, dogs don't need petting or comforting or treats. They need *direction* from you—a constructive thumbs-up or thumbs-down of their **behavior.**

If your pup is fearful rather than aggressive, should you correct that, too? Absolutely. A dog who is allowed to practice fearful behavior may escalate over time until he actually lashes out at an innocent person who startles him.

Shyness can be a serious behavior problem, especially in large breeds who can do a lot of damage if their anxiety leads to a defensive bite.

It's perfectly normal for a puppy to occasionally act worried about something he sees or hears. Just give the pup something else to focus on ("Sit" or "Heel") and calmly and methodically correct misbehaviors such as pulling on the leash or barking.

On the other hand, if you *reward* worried behavior with petting and soothing words, you will push what was a minor concern into phobic fear or aggression.

Many dogs have been *made* anxious or aggressive or neurotic when their owner enabled the pup's anxiety by...

- reassuring, petting, or giving treats when he acts anxious.

- tightening his leash to hold him close to you.

- picking him up (unless an off-leash dog is running straight toward you!)

> Again, those soothing responses simply encourage a puppy to repeat the anxious behavior that resulted in petting and fondling. **Remember, only reward what you want repeated.**

Socializing with other dogs

Here we run into the same basic issues as socializing with strangers.

1. Are you trying to make your puppy *more social* with other dogs (i.e., do you want him to be friendly and to play with other dogs?)

2. Or are you simply trying to teach him how to behave properly in a *social setting* that includes other dogs?

I favor #2. In my opinion, letting your pup play with other dogs that you don't know and can't control is very risky. It can take only one instance in which your puppy is attacked by another dog for him to start acting aggressively toward other dogs for the rest of his life. His mentality becomes, "I'll get them before they get me."

Owners consult with me all the time about these psychologically scarred dogs. "It was just that one time," they say mournfully.

Dog parks and dog beaches? Most own-ers stand around a dog park chatting, laugh-ing, and talking on their phones while their pup's body language (or some other dog's body language) is flashing bright red warning signs that a fight might be imminent.

I don't put my dogs' lives in the hands of other owners who don't recognize or respond properly to canine body language.

 Your dog doesn't need to play with other dogs in order to have a long and happy life. He really, really doesn't.

If you know the other dogs very well, that's fine. But it's more important that your pup learns how to share space with other dogs without flipping out, and to *pay attention to you* even when other dogs happen to be nearby.

 Other dogs who are being walked on a leash while you and your pup are also out on a walk.

 Other dogs who are in their own yards and happen to bark when you and your pup pass by.

 Other dogs who are sitting in the vet's office with their owner when you and your pup come in.

Those are the kinds of other dogs your puppy needs to be comfortable around. And by "comfortable," I don't mean that he needs to play with them. He just needs to accept them.

That means you correct any excitable, aggressive, or fearful behavior on his part. He needs to stand quietly beside you on a loose leash (Chapter 11).

If an off-leash dog approaches you on a walk

One of the responsibilities of a leader is to protect followers. When your puppy sees that *you* will step between him and an approaching dog, he will be more likely to relax when he sees other dogs. Often a pup who lunges at other dogs or bellows threats at other dogs is feeling anxious and insecure because he thinks *he* needs to handle potential threats.

So when you and your puppy go for a walk, especially in an area where you know other dogs run loose, take a sturdy walking stick.

If another dog actually approaches you and your puppy, step firmly between them. Brandish your walking stick and order the other dog to get lost. If he keeps coming, drive him away with a whack of your stick. If there is a truly aggressive dog in your area, carry pepper spray.

 When your pup witnesses that YOU are the leader and protector, he will feel less pressure to do this himself.

Should dogs be allowed to sniff each other?

I would need to know the other dog **very well.** Because if my pup is a small, sensitive, or timid dog, a mistake here could have catastrophic consequences to his future attitude toward other dogs.

More dog fights ensue from sniffing noses and butts than at any other time.

This canine ritual is where crucial *social signals* are exchanged. Each dog uses subtle body language to say things such as:

- "I'm the boss!"

- "Oh yeah? Says who?"

- "I don't like the way you look or smell."

- "I don't mean any harm, please don't hurt me!"

Dogs can carry on quite a sophisticated conversation using the positioning of their head, ears, and tail, the tension of their muscles, the "hardness" or "softness" of their facial expression.

When this exchange communicates a pecking order that both dogs agree with, everything will probably be fine. But if that order is in doubt, a fight will likely ensue, either immediately or soon.

> 🔅 The chances of a dog fight increase markedly when owners hold their dogs *on tight leashes* and let them sniff noses. Tight leashes lead to all kinds of behavior problems in dogs.

Even if an owner assures you that his dog is "good" with other dogs...

Take it with a grain of salt. Dog owners are always assuring people of their dog's "friendliness." Just ask any (bitten) vet, groomer, or mail carrier how many times he or she has been told, "Oh, my dog would never bite."

Sad to say, many owners know little or nothing about their own dog. Even worse, they have little or no control over its behavior.

Should you allow your small dog to play with a larger dog?

I don't. A larger dog can accidentally hurt a small dog simply by jumping up and down. Even a friendly head butt or playful pawing can harm or frighten a smaller dog.

And there is the *prey instinct* to think about.

I have been the unhappy eyewitness to horrifying spectacles in which a large dog suddenly grabbed, shook, and seriously injured (and in one tragic case, killed) the smaller one.

The speed with which it happens is unbelievable.

The problem is that larger dogs may view toy dogs as *prey*. A sudden movement, such as your toy dog pouncing on a leaf, can trigger chasing instincts even in a *nice* larger dog who means well. He can seize your little one before he even thinks about what he is doing—before you have time to move or draw a breath.

It has happened time and time again.

For safety's sake, if you own a small dog, assume that:

- Other owners don't understand the prey instinct.

- The efforts of other owners to control and restrain their dog may be slow, weak, and ineffective.

Chapter 44

Aggression and Reactivity Toward People or Other Dogs

Aggression is a complex behavioral issue, and there are different subtypes. For example,

- territorial/possessive/resource aggression—"This yard (toy, food, sofa, lap) is mine! Don't come near it." We've talked about resource guarding in previous chapters.

- dominant aggression—"*I'm* in charge! Don't cross me." This type of aggression is much less common that people think. When it does occur, it's usually toward other dogs rather than toward people.

- predatory aggression—powerful instincts to chase and grab things that move (cats, small dogs, livestock, bicycles). Dogs with a strong prey instinct don't have any malice toward the things they pursue or bite. They're just doing what primitive canines do—catching and killing things that run.

- reactive aggression. A *reactive* dog isn't truly possessive or dominant or predatory. Instead, he lives with a heightened sense of arousal where he overreacts to things in his environment that he misperceives as a threat. Reactive dogs are typically insecure, with a defensive mentality of "I'm gonna get *you* before you can get *me.*"

Living with a reactive dog

Along with possessive aggression (resource guarding), reactive aggression is a common behavior problem in dogs.

Suppose you're out for a walk and your pup spots another dog or person.

He charges to the end of the leash, lunging and growling and barking fiercely. He looks pretty aggressive, doesn't he?

But if he were suddenly let off leash (I'm NOT suggesting you do that!), would he run over and bite the other dog or person?

Surprisingly, most dogs would not. This is one of the signs of a reactive dog—he puts up a great front, but is too insecure to follow through. Even if he did charge the other dog or person, he usually retreats if his target stands its ground.

Whereas a truly dominant dog who is serious about his aggression is supremely confident and will readily attack other dogs or other people.

A *reactive* dog usually *reacts* only when something crosses his comfort line. Reactive dogs are typically anxious or frustrated, and they try to vent their anxiety or frustration with bursts of ferocity that are (mostly) bluff and bluster.

However, reactive dogs **can** bite if they feel pushed too far. But often they don't seem to realize they've done it until after the bite, and then they appear confused about what just happened.

> Owners don't help these dogs by holding them on a tight leash, which only makes a dog more stressed and frustrated.

You always want your pup on a loose leash. When you need to use the leash to correct your pup, do it rapidly—*pop* the leash—then loosen it again. If that doesn't work, switch to an alternative collar that does (Chapter 11).

I know it's stressful to go for a walk with a pup who acts aggressively toward other people or other dogs. You tense up whenever you see someone walking toward you.

The problem is, your dog can sense your anxiety and he thinks you're worried about *that approaching person*, which makes him even more likely to bellow threats.

So it's important to work on controlling your own anxiety. Slow your breathing and relax your muscles.

> Even more important, you need to put in place the proper leader-follower relationship at home. That means filling your puppy's daily life with structure and routines, requiring calmness indoors, consistently rewarding good behavior and correcting bad behavior, and controlling valued resources such as food, toys, and sleeping spots.

Proper leadership by itself can turn many reactive dogs around by relieving the dog's insecurity. Once he trusts his leader to handle and control everything in his life, a pup is more relaxed and less reactive.

What if a dog is aggressive toward his OWNER?

This usually doesn't appear until maturity (1 to 3 years old), when a dog's hormones blossom.

But the seeds of that aggression were actually planted in the dog's formative months.

Dogs most likely to bite their owners are those who, as youngsters, were allowed to guard their food or toys, demand petting, sleep on beds and furniture, jump on people, pull you around on the leash, resist grooming, rush through doors and gates ahead of you, and other disrespectful behaviors.

That pup grows up loving you lots, but respecting you hardly at all. So when you try to get the adult dog to do something he doesn't want to do, he resists, growls, or bites.

Dealing with aggression or reactivity issues

 Keep the dog's leash on. Dogs behaving poorly have not earned the privilege of freedom in your house. Either let the leash drag (when being monitored) or attach it to your waist so the pup must follow you around. Both physically and psychologically, this helps establish you as the leader and him as the follower.

 Insist upon calmness indoors—no barking, jumping, chasing, rough play, vigorous games, or racing around, *indoors* (Chapter 9).

 Several times a day, practice a quick (1-minute) program of words your pup knows. Again, this is good for building a proper leader-follower dynamic.

At least once a day, go for a short **structured** walk (Chapter 12). You'll probably need an alternative collar (Chapter 11).

 At least once a day, require your pup to stay quietly on his *Place* (Chapter 16) for an hour or two. Reactive dogs need to learn how to relax and do nothing.

 Follow a consistent leadership-based routine for mealtimes (Chapter 20).

 Don't allow the pup in the room where family members are eating. And not a single morsel of food from the table.

 Limit the dog's toys (Chapter 29).

 Keep the pup out of your bedroom. Not just off the bed— out of the bedroom entirely. He should sleep in a crate in another room. And no getting up on the furniture unless you invite him up **and send him off.** See Chapter 21.

 Randomly have the pup go into his crate and stay there for a short time until you let him out. Reactive dogs need to learn calmness and relaxation. See Chapter 13.

 Require him to *Sit* before you give a treat. Make sure he takes the food gently from your hand. See Chapter 19.

 Don't allow him to demand petting. You decide when to pet him, and not before having him do something (*Sit* or *Down* or *Place*).

Don't allow him to run through doors or gates—he must
Wait until you tell him he can go through (Chapter 15).

And if you think this is safe to do without being bitten...

 Teach the pup to accept handling all over his body
(Chapter 32).

Finally, learn the warning signs that a bite may be imminent.

People who have witnessed a biting incident often say, "It came
out of nowhere!" But virtually all dogs do give warning. You just need
to know what to look for.

Often these warning signs come over a period of time, in which
the dog becomes increasingly stressed by, for example, the excited
mannerisms of a child or the proximity of another dog.

Watch for these subtle signs that your pup is feeling stressed:

- Yawning

- Licking his lips

- The base of the ears pulled backward

- A worried or unhappy expression on the dog's face

- Closing his mouth and holding it closed and tense, whereas it
  had previously been open and relaxed

- Freezing in place, his body rigidly still

- Turning his head away from the thing that's stressing him (as
  though hoping that if he can't see it, it will go away)

Dogs who are possessive of their food bowl or a toy might hover their head low over the object, their front legs splayed out on either side, claiming and protecting it. The rest of their body is tense and rigid. These are dangerous signs that a bite is coming within a few seconds unless you back off.

Chapter 45

If You Have Children or Grandchildren

In this rather long chapter I cover:

 Getting a dog "for the kids"

 How often dogs bite children

 How to keep kids from being bitten by your dog

 Older children and dogs

 Infants and dogs

Getting a dog "for the kids"

The plan here is that the kids will come home from school and take the dog for a long walk and outside to play.

The problem is that most children don't interact with a dog in ways that encourage good habits. They don't create good routines, avoid bad routines, add rewards to good behavior, and correct bad behavior. Not consistently, anyway.

In fact, children can (unintentionally) undermine your attempts to raise a puppy to be well-behaved. Children tend to see dogs as furry playmates and will encourage the pup to do all sorts of undesirable things:

- Children will wrestle with the puppy with their hands, inciting him to struggle.

- They'll let the puppy pull on the leash and jump on them.

- They'll run away from the pup, inciting him to chase and nip.

- They'll stamp their foot playfully at the pup, inciting him to bark.

Mind you, none of this is done with bad intentions! Children who are having fun simply can't judge when a puppy is out of control and they can't correct a pup with enough authority when his behavior does go over the line.

Similarly, dogs tend to look at children as **littermates.** Dogs jump on children, grab things away from children, nip, chase, and play roughly, just as they would play with another dog.

Dogs don't view children as potential leaders to be respected—not until the child is mature enough to follow the instructions in this book. Typically that won't be until at least age 10 or so.

> 💡 You need to look at your children as honestly and objectively as possible. Are they mature enough and responsible enough to follow your rules of handling the puppy? If you tell them not to do something with the pup, will they stop doing it?

If not, they should not be allowed to interact with the puppy unless *you* are right there supervising.

But it's not just the *dog's* behavior you need to monitor—it's the kids' behavior too. Some owners think that it's entirely up to the dog to change his jumping or nipping behaviors even when the kids are egging him on. That isn't realistic or fair. The kids need to be taught what they are (and aren't) allowed to do, just as much as the dog does—often *more* than the dog does.

> 💡 If one or more of your kids can't or won't follow your instructions even when you're right beside them, the pup should be off limits until the child matures.

I realize this will be a great disappointment to parents who got the dog for the kids. And I'm sorry for needing to say it.

But a puppy is a living sponge soaking up all the undesirable things the kids are allowing him to do. From the kids, he will learn that rowdy, impulsive behaviors are allowed...and there is no behavior more rowdy and impulsive than a sudden bite.

How often dogs bite children

Regrettably, it's time for a few statistics:

- In the United States alone, **4 million people each year** are bitten by a dog. Nearly 500,000 require emergency room treatment, and 10,000 are hospitalized.

- About **two-thirds of bite victims** are children, mostly under the age of 12.

- **70% of dog bite injuries to children** under age 10 are to the face, often damaging the eyes or requiring major reconstructive surgery. Some children, including sleeping infants, are killed by dogs.

- **Over 50% of bitten children are bitten by the family's own dog.** Another 25% are bitten by a dog owned by a friend or relative. So even though we tell our kids, "Never pet a strange dog," the much more serious threat is inside our own home or over at the neighbor's.

> I've been working with dogs for over 40 years and love them dearly. But I respect that they have strong jaws and teeth. I hope you'll have that kind of healthy respect, as well.

Dogs don't always know that a child is human

You and I see children as human beings who are simply younger and smaller than adults. But from the perspective of many dogs, young children are nothing like adult human beings.

Young children move their arms and legs with unpredictable, herky-jerky movements. Young children bump into things, drop things, knock things over. They trip and fall. They jump up and down, hit and kick things, yell and cry in high-pitched voices.

> From a dog's perspective, a child (especially a young child, up to about age 10) is a very different creature than you are.

How to keep kids from being bitten by your dog

1) Choose a dog who is good-natured and easygoing.

Avoid dogs with a strong prey instinct that compels them to chase and grab things that move. Avoid dogs who are shy, sensitive, or easily startled. Avoid possessive dogs who guard their food or toys. You can find temperament tests in my dog buying guide, *Dog Quest.* If you're getting a young puppy, you need to evaluate the temperament of both parents.

If your kids are under the age of 8 or 9, avoid toy breeds. Many children are bitten when attempting to pick up a tiny breed, or pat the top of its head, which looks threatening (understandably!) to a small dog.

2) Raise your dog properly.

 Make sure you and your spouse are the leaders in your household. Your pup should be a well-behaved follower. A dog who sees himself as a leader feels justified in disciplining/biting a lower-ranking group member who does something the dog doesn't like.

 Maintain your pup's health and grooming so he isn't in chronic pain or discomfort. A dog who hurts feels irritable and could lash out if a child did something that made the pain worse. Painful health issues include untreated hip dysplasia, bad teeth, matted hair, or an ear infection.

 Don't tie your puppy outside or leave him unsupervised in the yard where he can run up and down the fence barking. Tied dogs and fence runners often bite from frustration.

 Don't allow your pup to practice excitable behaviors such as jumping or rough play. Families with kids need a calm dog.

3) Raise your *kids* properly. Don't allow a child to:

- hug a dog (this can make him feel trapped)
- kiss a dog, or put her face near a dog's face
- stare into a dog's eyes
- touch a dog when he's sleeping or looking in another direction
- climb onto a dog's back
- approach a dog when he's eating or chewing on a bone
- try to take something away from a dog

- chase a dog

- make barking or growling sounds at a dog

- stamp her foot at a dog, even playfully

- yell or scream around a dog

It's astonishing that some parents allow crazy behaviors, such as letting a child sit on the dog or crawl over to his food bowl while he's eating. "My dog tolerates anything," a parent might claim proudly. "He would never bite."

I'm sorry, but that's bad parenting of the child and bad leadership of the dog. You're supposed to be the guardian, the protector, of both of them.

That means you don't put either of them in harm's way, the classic "accident waiting to happen."

> Emergency room personnel can tell you how many toddlers have been bitten by the family dog and how many parents lament, "But he never did that before. What happened?" What happened is that the dog had had enough. Dogs are not benevolent grandparents. They view the world through canine eyes and they speak very effectively with their teeth.

I should mention that the **no-no list** above—what children should **not** do with a dog—also applies to any child who visits your home (nieces and nephews, grandchildren, and neighborhood kids who come over to play with yours).

If a child in your home or yard won't follow your instructions about what they can and cannot do with your puppy, then (1) the child needs to leave or (2) your pup needs to be put someplace that's off limits to the kids.

Older children and dogs

When can a child interact with your puppy without supervision? Obviously, age can't be a hard-and-fast dividing line. It would be silly to declare that a child who is 9 years and 11 months old isn't old enough… but a child who is exactly 10 years old is!

Still, around age 10 or so is a reasonable dividing line, simply because many children around age 10 change their mannerisms and body language enough that dogs can recognize them as smaller versions of humans. This simple change in perception—by the **DOG**—can help decrease the incidence of dog bites that are related to the dog not recognizing the child as a human.

In addition, children around this age are better able to understand that their behaviors have consequences, so they're more likely to be consistent in behaving properly around dogs.

But you need to look carefully at your individual child. If your 11-year-old is still quite childish (loud, boisterous, clumsy, or likes to roughhouse), don't trust him with unsupervised canine care. Give him more time to mature.

> *Once kids are mature enough,* they can be amazingly tuned-in to a dog and can often handle the dog better than grown-ups!

Babies and dogs

You may have heard that "dogs instinctively know how to treat a baby gently."

That's not true. Many dogs are uncomfortable around babies. Many dogs don't even realize that a baby is human. Dogs have killed babies, even sleeping babies.

Yet parents will pose their infants with the family dog in insane ways, with the infant propped against the side of the dog's head, or "riding" the dog like a pony. I know these parents mean well, but it shows a lack of understanding and respect for canine thought processes and canine teeth.

Of course, ultimately it's up to you how much contact you allow your pup to have with your baby. But I can tell you what's safer and what's riskier.

The safest way to have both a dog and an infant is to make it clear to the dog that the baby is *your* possession, protected by *you.* For quite some time, you don't allow the pup to touch the baby or even enter the baby's nursery.

For example, you can teach your pup to "Wait" (Chapter 15) just outside the door to the nursery without crossing the threshold.

Once he is doing well with this lesson and won't enter the room, you can start giving him permission ("Okay") to come in and sniff around a bit. You want him to learn that this special room is *yours* and that *you* decide if and when he can enter.

Next, you can push the baby in a carriage as you take the pup for a walk. He should walk *beside* you and *behind* the stroller. The pup learns that he follows both of you. If you haven't yet taught your dog to walk properly on a leash so that he will stay behind the stroller, you need to work on that (Chapter 11) before walking the baby and dog together.

When should you allow the pup to actually touch the baby with his nose? to lick the baby? There's no definitive answer to such questions. If you can control your pup at all times, you might start giving him the "Okay" to come closer to the baby.

Chapter 46

If You Have Other Dogs

Suppose you already have a dog, or several dogs, and you bring home a new puppy.

A multi-dog household can be one of the easiest—*or most diffi-cult*—environments in which to raise and train a new puppy. Everything depends on what those other dogs are like!

If your other dogs are calm, well-behaved, and respectful of you and of each other...

> congratulations! You've succeeded in establishing the right social dynamic, and a new puppy is likely to follow and adopt their behavior. In essence, the other dogs will demonstrate, through their body language and attentiveness to you, that they respect YOU as the leader. The new pup is likely to copy them and do the same thing.

But if your other dogs have behavioral issues...

> if they jump on people, bicker with each other, aren't 100% housebroken, or only listen to you when they feel like it...well, a new puppy is likely to follow unruly dogs into misbehavior. You should have waited until you succeeded

in establishing the right relationship with your existing dogs first.

> If your existing dogs are misbehaving, you should spend as much time working with them as you do with the new one.

Dog-on-dog aggression

My fellow trainers and I are frequently called into multi-dog households that are in chaos.

Dogs are sociable animals. When they join our family, they seek to find out its structure. Who are the leaders and who are the followers? Introducing a new pup into an established canine group **changes** the group dynamic. Sometimes the dogs are so good-natured that there are no issues. But sometimes fights break out when the dogs disagree about the new pecking order.

While a new dog is just a puppy, fights seldom happen, because most adult dogs have some natural tolerance toward a puppy.

But when the pup matures (between 1 and 3 years of age), all of the dogs suddenly want to know, "Who's in charge? Which dogs can I pick on? Which dogs are going to pick on me?" And all hell may break loose. Owners are often shocked by this.

Dog-on-dog aggression *within a family* can be one of the most difficult behavior problems to solve because it requires a particular kind of owner who can "read" dogs accurately and recognize the most subtle signs of a pending confrontation. Sometimes two dogs must be kept separated forever, or one of them re-homed, preferably into a household with no other dogs.

How to avoid problems in multi-dog households

Rule #1: All of your dogs must act like equals.

No dog should be allowed to dominate any other dog. The only one in charge is **YOU** (and the other adult humans).

Forget ideas like "letting the dogs work it out" or shrugging off a fight with the excuse like "He's the boss of the other dogs."

YOU are the only one who should be the boss. All of your dogs should conduct themselves as equals. Whether you have two dogs or ten, they're equals. If any dog tries to take advantage of another dog, you step in right away and stop it.

Don't allow one dog to pester another. Often a puppy will persistently try to play with an older dog who is trying to sleep. Puppies should be on a leash, not free to wander around the house pestering other dogs.

Don't allow one dog to take anything away from another. That includes toys, food, and beds. If a dog is chewing peacefully on a toy, or eating his food, or sleeping on a dog bed, the other dogs must not try to take it away or intimidate the first dog away from it.

> **You need to protect every dog from being jumped on, chased, teased, bullied, or simply overwhelmed by children or other pets.** Trust me, dogs *notice* when you step in and stop the jumping, chasing, bullying, etc. They also notice when you just sprawl in a chair watching TV and fail to keep them safe.

Don't allow any dog to discipline another dog. That's *your* job. If a dog is chewing on a toy and another dog tries to take it away and the first dog lunges to fight, **you** discipline BOTH dogs. Put the toy away and send both dogs to their crates or to their "Places." The *Place* command is taught in Chapter 16.

The only time I relax this rule that "I am the only one who disciplines" is when a puppy is pestering an older dog, and before I can get over there to stop the puppy, the older dog growls or snaps, perhaps even making the puppy yelp but not harming him.

This is a *canine social signal* and it's important for Puppy to understand. So I don't discipline the older dog—hopefully he taught Puppy a valuable lesson.

Still, you don't want this to become a pattern. If Puppy doesn't get the message, if instead he goes right back to pestering, put him on a leash or in his crate or pen, before things escalate and he gets bitten much harder…and then you would need to discipline the older dog, as well.

Rule #2: All of your dogs must get equal time and attention.

When you first see your dogs in the morning, or after coming home from work or shopping, greet them individually by name.

Look at each dog as you give him an affectionate pat or a quick rub of his head and ears. Then move on to the next dog.

Dogs love patterns, so I always greet (and feed) my dogs in the order I got them. The dog who has lived with me the longest gets the first greeting, and the newest dog gets the last greeting.

Jealousy is not allowed. If you're petting one dog, another dog may not try to interrupt. If a dog is pushy and tries to shove his way forward for more petting, or for petting out of turn, keep your hands off him and ignore him until last. Then have him "Sit" before he gets his attention.

Also make time for all of your dog(s) *as individuals.* Take one dog for a walk—just the two of you. Take one dog to the basement for 10 minutes of brushing—just the two of you. Play a game of fetch with just one dog.

Having you all to himself sometimes is important to a dog. And it's just as important that the other dog(s) recognize that **you** make the decisions about *who* gets attention and *when.* It's a subtle leadership thing.

Chapter 47

If You Have a Cat

Most dog-cat problems are related to chasing. Even when done for fun, chasing games played indoors keep a dog in a heightened state of arousal, which is the opposite of the calm behavior you're trying to instill for daily living.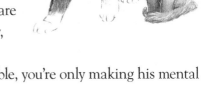

Now, if your dog is already calm and well-behaved, and if he and the cat are good friends who play together nicely, that's fine.

But if your dog tends to be excitable, you're only making his mental state more aroused if you allow him to chase or roughhouse with the cat.

Suppose you already have a cat and you're adding a new puppy to your family.

 If the puppy is large, strong, and older, your primary concern is protecting the *cat.*

If the pup is small and young, your primary concern is protecting the *pup.* A cat's claws can blind a clumsy puppy or small dog whose face is down around the cat's level.

 Your secondary concern is establishing the rule that *calmness is required* inside your house.

You'll remember from Chapter 9 (calmness) that when you bring home a new puppy, you shouldn't allow him loose indoors. He should be in a crate or pen, or on a leash, until he is 100% housebroken and well-behaved.

Remember, we're not just concerned with safety here. **We also want calmness.** If a pup can't remain perfectly calm when he's crated or leashed and the cat strolls past, how is he likely to act when he's *not* crated or *not* leashed?

Keeping your puppy under control means he can become accustomed to the presence of the cat at the same time as he is learning the rules in your household.

> The vast majority of dogs will then leave the cat alone, *simply because you say so.* This is why leadership is so important. Once you have it, raising and training a dog is not difficult.

Here's another cat-readiness test: put the cat in a plastic crate/carrier on the floor. Attach your pup's leash but drop your end so he can drag it. Stand across the room and wait until your puppy is nosing at the crate. Then call him. Does he come?

> If you can't call your pup away from a passive cat in a carrier, what are you going to do if the cat is loose and there is a wild chase?

Establishing leadership takes time. Teaching a reliable **Come** command takes time. Don't be in a hurry to combine cat and dog!

Suppose you have the PUPPY first and you're adding a cat to your family...how do you introduce them?

First, you shouldn't add a cat to your family until you have enough voice control over your dog that you can say "No" and he immediately stops what he's doing **AND** until you can say "Come" and he always comes.

If your puppy is like that, introducing a new cat is quite easy. The cat should be in charge. By that, I mean the cat should determine, with her hisses and swipes, how close the pup is allowed to come. When the cat recognizes her own power and the dog accepts it, there should be very few problems.

Can every dog live safely with a cat?

Unfortunately not. There are some dogs who never accept that the cat is in charge. Typically these are dogs with strong prey instincts. For example, working or hunting lines of Belgian Malinois, Rottweilers, German Shepherds, American Bulldogs, German Pointers, Airedales, and similar breeds.

Sighthounds (such as Borzois) and *northern "spitz" breeds* such as Alaskan Malamutes and Akitas can also have prey drives that are too high for cat (or small dog) safety.

Now if such a dog is well-trained and respectful, he might control his prey drive in your presence. But leaving that dog alone with the cat will never be completely safe.

> If you ever find yourself *hoping* that things might be okay, don't leave them alone together! Don't take chances with the lives of vulnerable pets who depend on you to protect them.

What if the CAT is the aggressive one?

If your cat is actually attacking or teasing your puppy mercilessly, correct her in no uncertain terms with a spray of water from a squirt gun or spray bottle.

As your pup's leader, one of your responsibilities is to step in and protect him from other animals. Believe me, your pup notices when you stand up for him. He also notices when you ignore the situation. Don't let him down.

Chapter 48

Abused Dogs

"What about abuse? My dog is a rescue dog and he's afraid of men, so he was probably abused…"

It's common for dog lovers to suspect abuse when a dog is fearful or aggressive. And of course there are dogs out there who have been hit, or beaten.

But it's far more common that if abuse occurred at all, it was *psychological*, not physical. In other words, it isn't so much what DID happen to him, as what DIDN'T happen but should have.

For example:

- **Lack of socialization.** Dogs are less likely to be confident about the world if they weren't taken out into the world, during their formative months, to see lots of new things. So they react with suspiciousness, skittishness, or aggression because they don't have the foundational confidence that would have been instilled by proper exposure to the world.

- **Lack of leadership.** When a dog encounters something in the world that makes him feel concerned, his leader needs to immediately step in and show the dog how to behave in that situation. No nervous woofing allowed. No barking or lunging allowed. Loose leash required. Calmness required. If the owner doesn't provide that guidance and direction, the dog feels alone and might react in the only ways he knows how— the classic *fight or flight* response. As the poor leadership continues, the dog becomes more and more anxious, fearful, or aggressive.

- **And then there are bad genes.** Dogs can inherit what we call "weak nerves" or hyper-reactivity to normal sights, sounds, and movements. These dogs are quick to startle or flinch. Some cower, or shiver and shake, when they see or hear something that other dogs handle with confidence. Unfortunately, *genetic* shyness or anxiety is more difficult to fix because you can't change the genes the dog inherited.

Physical abuse is not as common as you think, so don't hold onto your speculation that your dog "must have been abused" as an excuse to let him keep acting aggressive or fearful. **At this point, the cause doesn't matter.**

> Dogs aren't into psychoanalysis, and feeling sorry for a dog's past doesn't help him at all. His past is over. Move forward. Let him know, with consistent rewards and corrective techniques, which behaviors you want and which behaviors are unacceptable. *Calm leadership* is what your pup wants and needs, no matter what his "back story" is. *Calm leadership* is the ultimate way to show your pup that you love him. That's what this book is all about.

Index

Made in the USA
Las Vegas, NV
09 November 2021